salt & ash & honey & magic

JAMIE ELIZABETH METZGAR

This book is dedicated to William Keith Metzgar & Klaus Ernest Mason Metzgar.
Are there any creatures who delight in each other as much as we three?
ILYAIAW.

And to everyone else we lost way too soon:
Joe Maciejewski, Matt Herold, Kathy Kane, Warren Barbour, Michael Smith and Myrna Donahoe.

table of contents

foreward

This time last year, writing a book about loss and grief was the last thing on my mind. But then within six months my husband Bill died, my mother had heart surgery, and our dog Klaus was killed. As I struggled to deal with the emotional overload, I poured all of my energy into renovating our dream house. But even this experience quickly turned into a nightmare, as I confronted living somewhere where both my husband and dog died. It was, to say the least, a lot.

In the aftermath of these events, what became apparent was how few resources there are for those of us widowed on the younger side of life. Most support groups assumed that both partners were retired and with adult children. Neither was true for me, nor did I ascribe to a specific faith. I relied heavily on loved ones, on nature, and on my own physical strength. Bill loved my spirit and independence and for me to crumble seemed a massive disservice to him.

Losing my family felt like I was punched right out of my life and into a gaping cosmic ocean. I fought to regain my stability, but would get pulled right back under by the next wave of loss. Eventually, I learned to drift along and pay attention to the universe until I was back on solid ground.

Spending so much time alone allows plenty of time to think, and I found that my perspective shifted significantly in the wake of my loss.

This book is about coming to interpret life as equal parts salt, ashes, honey, and magic. Salt enhances flavor, it preserves, but too much of it is corrosive and overpowering. Ashes are the remains after destruction, but ashes can be used to help fertilize new growth. Honey is the result of diligence and, although we use it for sweetness, its primary function is to nourish and sustain the hive. And magic is everything else; everything we don't understand and never will.

Life is understanding and appreciating this balance.

salt

/sôlt/

noun

a white crystalline substance which gives seawater its characteristic taste and is used for seasoning or preserving food.

something which adds freshness or piquancy.

INFORMAL
an experienced sailor.

rub salt into the wound
make a painful experience even more painful for someone.

the salt of the earth
a person or group of people of great kindness, reliability, or honesty.

worth one's salt
good or competent at the job or profession specified.

01

I sometimes wonder if, deep down, Bill and I both knew something bad was going to happen. I feel like there were signs that I must have noticed, because my mind kept running back to things that we both left incomplete.

We moved out to California in 2015, one year after we'd gotten married. After moving several times, we landed in the Bay Area. Bill was determined to buy property as a retirement investment for me, but Bay Area prices were astronomical. After much searching, we found the perfect place for us and our scruffy little dog, Klaus. It was in Lake County, just north of Napa. We bought it in July 2018 and began commuting back and forth to the Bay Area.

By March 2019, the commute was growing on us and we made the decision to move up there permanently. I planned to make the case to my boss in April during my annual review. I figured that if my team of all-remote workers handled the holidays without a problem, I could certainly work remotely as well. Meanwhile, Bill quit his part time job and planned to begin his transition up to the house. But something kept holding us back and neither of us could articulate what. He claimed to be worried about money but when I asked him why, there was no pressing reason.

As we wavered about the move, I couldn't stop thinking about our trip to Barcelona the year before. It was one of the best trips we ever took together. We didn't have a firm plan and instead spent our days exploring the city on foot and finding some fantastic spots. In our seven years together we'd been to nine countries and countless cities around the States, and we both fell more in love with Barcelona than anywhere else we'd been. Bill even talked about moving there, something he'd never done before. But as the trip drew to a close, I felt an incredible sadness settle into my chest.

On our last night there, I wrote in my journal "I feel like this is the last time we'll be in Europe." It didn't make any sense, because there was nothing to prevent us from going back. Later it occurred to me that it meant our last time together as a couple.

Bill had always been so self-conscious of our age difference. He would worry that I'd grow tired of him, of being seen with an old man. It never bothered me in the least and I tried to reassure him of that. I told him we had plenty of similar tastes despite the twenty years between us. But in that last year together, I noticed that if something came up that he wasn't sure he could do – like a hike – he'd just give a hard no to it and that was that.

When it was time to plan our vacation for 2019, Bill insisted he didn't want to travel without our dog Klaus anymore. Klaus was getting older and we needed to spend as much time as we could with him. I agreed and we planned a cross-country adventure, driving from Oakland to New York and back. We bought a Jeep and I pieced together an itinerary that we both loved.

But something told me not to book it. Bill asked me a few times when I was going to make reservations and I said as soon as I got back from Miami, but I wonder if I knew even then that the trip wasn't going to happen. Maybe Bill also knew. He seemed fixated on my safety and had been obsessed with replacing my Fiat, which was just fine, with something more reliable. We went with the Jeep because it was stable and sturdy.

Sunday, March 3rd was his last day at work. He was going to semi-retire and transition up to the house. I went to the gym that morning and when I came home I saw his car parked out front. I went into a cold panic because he wasn't supposed to be home for several hours. I ran into the house to find him back in bed saying that he had left early because he didn't feel well. He wouldn't elaborate other than saying he felt dizzy and his arm was numb. I asked him if he wanted to go to the ER and he insisted he did not. When I pressed him, he said "Stop nagging me! You're stressing me out even more!" It was so unlike him to snap. He insisted he would be fine. Klaus was nestled in with him.

On Monday he said he felt better. I asked him to please go see his doctor but he said there was no reason to.

On Tuesday, March 5th, I woke up to learn my friend Claudia's brother had died suddenly. I was shocked. I'd been friendly with him over the years; we had even gone to Claudia's wedding together. I fumbled through offering my condolences. Bill shook his head and asked how their mother was holding up.

That afternoon we went to an industry tasting together. He seemed completely fine. But "the saddest words in English are 'You're gone'" kept echoing in my mind. I thought it was about Matt.

On Wednesday, he made a kickass Latin-inspired dinner in honor of my work trip to Miami, where I would be attending a trade show. He told me he was proud of me and excited for me. It took him a long time to fall asleep that night, but he was finally out when I got up early the morning of Thursday, March 7th to go to the airport. I didn't want to disturb him so I called an Uber. I woke him to say goodbye right as I was leaving, and I felt that sadness in my chest again as I left.

On the way to the airport "Marry You" by Bruno Mars came on the radio and I smiled because it was the song Bill played right before proposing to me.

He died eight hours later.

02

My favorite colleague and I were halfway through dinner when I excused myself to use the bathroom and casually looked at my phone. I saw a text from Aaron, who lived on our property and took care of it when we weren't there. It simply read "Please call me." I knew something awful had happened but I tried to stay calm.

"Bill collapsed..." Aaron said on the phone. "The ambulance was here right away and he's at the hospital. Here's the phone number..."

And then we were at the airport and I was trying desperately to get a flight home. Aaron had assured me that Bill was alive when the EMTs arrived. On the phone, the hospital nurse kept referring to Bill in the present tense. I just wanted to be there by his side. It was too late, I was told, there were no flights out to California. The airline clerk scanned all of the other airlines leaving out of Miami that night. Nothing was available.

And then the doctor called and said "Mrs. Metzgar... I'm so sorry." What? Sorry about what? "We couldn't revive him. We worked on him for an hour."

"Why did you let me hope?" I asked.

Back in my hotel room, I had to somehow get through the night. I knew I should start calling people, but I didn't know where to begin. My mind felt like it had been seared by a white-hot iron. There were big stretches of blank expanse. I remember trying to call people, trying to sleep, but only being able to double over in pain.

I called our landlord, Dom. We'd become friends with Dom in the year and a half that we lived in his Oakland cottage, often having dinner together or chatting during the day. We would joke that Klaus was his puppy's uncle.

"Can you talk?"

"We're just about to have dinner... can I call you back in an hour?"

"No, please, it's important."

"Hey," he said, his voice soothing, "What's going on?"

"Bill died."

I couldn't say any more than that. I heard Dom gasp. "Where are you?"

"Miami," I said, and then I broke down completely. How the fuck could I be in Miami when my husband had just died?! Was this really happening?

I could hear Dom weeping on the other end of the phone. He kept asking what he could do and I kept saying nothing. There was nothing to be done.

"Can we pick you up at the airport tomorrow?" he asked.

I said yes.

I made it to dawn. I remember an unquenchable thirst. It turns out that weeping is severely dehydrating, which wasn't something I'd ever considered before. I went through every bottle the hotel had set out, which I believe was four.

Back at the airport, I don't remember checking in or security or boarding. I do remember the flight attendant's reaction to my face, and she treated me delicately. I wept the entire flight.

By the time I landed, I had about ten Facebook messages. I couldn't understand how people had already found out, but then I saw that two of Bill's close family members had posted about his death and tagged me. I felt like I'd been punched in the gut. I was absolutely not prepared to talk to so many people just yet. In the middle of the San Francisco airport, I logged into Facebook and wrote:

I apologize in advance for not replying individually to messages and I apologize further if this is how you're finding out. Bill passed away last night at our house in Clearlake. I am beyond devastated and have no idea what will happen next. If you knew Bill at all, you know he had a heart as big as his world and that's just somehow gone. Please know that I've read all of your messages and so deeply appreciate them. Xoxo.

After I clicked "post," I breathed out and realized I had been unable to take a deep breath since the night before.

As I made my way to the exit, my stomach tightened up. What would I say to Dom? He was so loving and gracious, but I couldn't even think much less talk. The sun seemed unnaturally bright. I found Dom's car and climbed into the back. His puppy jumped into my lap. I hugged her tightly and cried into her fur. All of my hesitations evaporated and I realized: you don't need to do anything right now.

03

Through the haze and pain of those 24 hours, it gradually dawned on me that Bill was gone. There was no goodbye, no explanation. It felt like I had been blindsided by the universe and left speechless and disoriented. It was a hell that I was only beginning to enter.

Our cottage in Oakland was unnaturally silent. Klaus was still up at our house in Lake County. I walked into our bedroom. Bill's flannel shirt was hanging on a hook. His book was tossed carelessly onto his nightstand. How was he just gone?

Our friend Becky met me at the cottage. We had met her back east, and she'd moved to Oakland around the same time we did. I asked her to help me go through all of Bill's papers. Since it was early March, he'd been putting paperwork together to bring to our tax accountant. I'd assumed it would be organized, because all of our bills were paid on time and he was adamant about not paying interest. Instead, I found random papers haphazardly tossed together. I realized he wasn't organized; he just knew where everything was in his own inscrutable system.

I began to understand how many basic things I didn't know how to do. I've heard a lot of women express anger towards their late partners for being suddenly abandoned, as irrational as that may seem. I did not experience this at all because any anger I held was reserved for one person and one person alone: me.

How could I, at 44, not know our financial situation? Why didn't I know how to make bread? How could I not know who our accountant was? And why in god's name could I not even reach the top shelf in my own kitchen?

My identity was rocked. I had prided myself on our marriage and our little family with Klaus. I felt so incredibly stupid and naïve for never considering that I'd be on my own. I just always assumed Bill would be there.

Our house! I thought. Did he have a will? He'd talked about writing one but did he ever finish? If not, would I lose the house? Would I be considered his beneficiary for anything?

My mother arrived in Oakland the same day I arrived home. Becky stayed with me and volunteered to pick her up. I was barely standing from exhaustion by then, but I knew I wouldn't be able to sleep.

When my mother walked in, I could tell by her expression that I looked like hell.

We drove up to the house on Sunday, March 10th. It was a long drive and it gave my mother time to make a list of everything I needed to do. The next day, at her insistence, I went to see Bill's body at the mortuary.

He was laid out, his head wrapped up. I was warned that since he'd fallen face-down, there would be some bruising. I wanted to start screaming for him to come back.

I touched his hair lightly. I always loved his hair because it was so soft.

At the sheriff's office, the coroner met with me. "Was it a heart attack?" I asked. She nodded. "The kind that just drops you. He never knew what hit him." I suppose I was relieved, but I still was in such shock. The only comfort at all was knowing that the last thing he saw was Klaus playing in the yard.

After collecting Bill's wallet and wedding ring, my mother said she was hungry. We stopped for lunch. As we got out of my car, I noticed that she had an odd expression on her face and was walking slowly. We sat, and she finally said, "I'm not feeling well."

"What?" I asked. "How?"

"I'm lightheaded and dizzy. I didn't want to tell you this, but I need to have heart surgery."

"Do you need to go to a hospital?"

She paused for a moment, then nodded. "Yes. Yes, I think so."

"Get up. Let's go."

"Don't you want to have lunch?" she asked.

I almost laughed at the absurdity of the question. "No," I said. "I want you to not die instead."

My brain was frozen as we started driving toward the hospital by my house. About halfway there, she said she felt better and didn't want to go. I asked "Are you sure?" about twenty times, but she insisted.

My mother needed heart surgery. I struggled to process this. She told me it was scheduled for May. When I could, I would book tickets and a hotel so I could be there with her. I sequestered that thought to the back of my mind. I couldn't handle my immediate grief if I allowed this to compound it.

04

I used to joke that my preferred weight loss methods were heartache and food poisoning because I'd be in awful pain for a week and viola: five pounds gone! Stressful events cause me to lose my appetite completely. I last maybe two bites if I manage to eat at all and beyond that, I feel nauseous. It feels like my body is already full of emotion and I need to digest that first.

It's powerful to respect how my body was trying to handle the onslaught of pain and trauma and allow it the space to do so. I realized I had to take a step back and just listen to what my body was attempting to tell me. To force myself to eat was pointless and only left me feeling even more exhausted.

I also noticed that my posture changed. I am not a tall person - I'm 5'4" if we round up - but people usually think I'm taller because of how I carry myself. But as I struggled with my grief, I found that I couldn't sit up straight. Any time I tried to straighten up, fear resonated along my sternum and my shoulders drew in again. It felt like my body was trying to protect me against a further blow - and, as it turned out, that blow would come later in the year.

My mother left after a few days and Bridget arrived. I'd known Bridget for about ten years and she had lived with Bill and me for a while in New York. Bill loved her as much as I did. He called her "our little Brigitte" and enjoyed telling her stories from his past. Bridget adopted our cat when we moved, which is a much bigger undertaking than it sounds like because Colette is semi-feral and barely tolerates most people.

Klaus had been on high alert since Bill died but I hadn't noticed it until Bridget arrived. Klaus wouldn't let her inside of the Oakland cottage and nipped her hand when she tried. I realized that he was being protective of me since Bill was gone.

We made our way up to the house in Lake County and Bridget went with me to pick up Bill's ashes. To see what was left of my husband in a big plastic box was absurd and terrible.

The mortuary director explained the complicated laws about transporting ashes and then gave me two certificates, one in my name and one in Bill's daughter Leah's name. She was going to arrive in a few weeks for a small memorial we were holding and she would take half of his ashes with her back to New York. How cold it seemed to think about portioning out his ashes.

As we were leaving, he said, "Want to hear something weird? Our ashes are usually within a half-pound of what we weighed at birth." I thought, "What the fuck did that human just say to me?" but I nodded and turned away. When we got to my car, I saw Bridget looked just as stunned as I was and we both burst out laughing.

Bridget was the perfect friend to be with me. She didn't expect to be entertained and she understood that I was a mess. We stayed at the house for a few days and visited a nearby winery. Before she left, she made up some witchy little charm packets and buried them around the yard for protection. I wish they had worked.

| 05

When I was in Oakland, Dom checked in on me constantly. His wife brought me two shopping bags full of groceries, which was both kind and astute because I was having a very difficult time holding it together in public. Dom would often come stand with me in the yard and watch the dogs play together in comforting silence.

About two weeks after Bill died, Dom invited me to a sound bath. He'd mentioned them before, but I was a spiritual skeptic and shrugged off most things that weren't concrete. When he suggested it this time, I was so desperate for relief from the pain that I went.

It was a profound experience. Dom talked us through a short relaxation meditation before beginning the sound bath using crystal bowls. I let myself melt into it and felt a calm for the first time since the day Bill died. Dom told us to pay attention to any colors we might notice during the experience. I kept seeing bits of green and violet. When I told Dom, he smiled and said "Green is the heart chakra."

As I was leaving, a hummingbird hovered in front of me for almost a full minute before zipping away.

I was unprepared for the terrible silence. Bill and I had been in constant contact since we'd started dating seven years before. We usually spoke several times throughout our workday and texted when we couldn't talk. The day he died, we had talked as soon as I landed in Miami and texted before I went to dinner. To go from such consistent communication to nothing was awful. There were so many things I wanted to tell him. I often picked up my phone to text him before I remembered I couldn't. I missed the sound of the gate swinging open when he came home, I missed the sound of Klaus racing out to meeting him, I missed his cheerful "Hiya, toots!" I missed everything.

But I felt suffocated by his possessions. His laundry was still in the hamper and I started washing it, only to realize afterward that it was pointless. A few times, I cried into one of his flannels. But after a few weeks, I moved all of his belongings to his side of the closet.

Towards the end of March, we had a small memorial up at the house. Bill's daughter Leah and her husband Casey flew in from New York. There were friends and family from Southern California and the Bay Area. One of his former students flew in from Minnesota for it. One of Bill and Aaron's colleagues from the wine shop handed me a bottle of Muller-

Catoir Riesling. "She doesn't like Riesling," Aaron told him, but I knew why: Bill and I went to Muller-Catoir in Germany and it was one of the few Rieslings I loved. I was so touched that he had remembered.

Leah and I buried some of Bill's ashes at the base of two pear trees he had planted three months before for our anniversary. I was grateful that so many people had come to Lake County to show love for Bill. As I went to bed that night, my mind shifted from "I don't want to do this without you" to "Please help me get through this." I knew I could draw from the love for Bill to help support me and figure out what the hell to do with the rest of my life.

06

For the next few months I drove up to our house every Friday morning, leaving before dawn to get there in time to start my workday. I didn't mind waking up early, and I loved having the quiet time with Klaus curled up on the passenger seat. It was a beautiful drive, especially when the sun rose as I came into Napa Valley.

In the beginning of April, I pulled out into the street and realized something was horribly wrong. My Jeep felt like it was dragging a grand piano and there was an awful screeching noise. I pulled over and parked. When I got out, I saw that the driver's side rear wheel was tilted in. I could not, for the life of me, figure out what the hell had happened. We'd just bought the car two months earlier – did the axel break? Was that even a thing? Why did I know nothing about cars?! Then I noticed that the wheel hub was badly dented, something I had missed in the dim morning light. Someone had hit my car and taken off.

I found our insurance cards. An agent named Rick answered and after a few questions about what happened, he asked what our deductible was. I burst out crying. I had no idea. Bill had always handled it. I wept over the phone as I explained everything. "Please don't worry," he told me, "I'll take care of everything."

He did, but it took a month before my car was completely repaired. Meanwhile, it was one more thing to stress about -- schlepping between rental car companies and body shops, maintaining two households, work, and giving Klaus the love he needed. I began to fear every morning because it felt like each day brought a fresh hell.

For the next few months I drove up to our house every Friday morning, leaving before dawn to get there in time to start my workday. I didn't mind waking up early, and I loved having the quiet time with Klaus curled up on the passenger seat. It was a beautiful drive, especially when the sun rose as I came into Napa Valley.

⸻

As I tried to handle life without Bill, I jumped back in to work. I managed a team of online wine experts at a national retailer. The company was fantastic to me and I loved my coworkers, who were knowledgeable, warm, funny, and caring. We all supported each other despite never having met.

The director of Human Resources told me to take as much time as I needed to without worrying about using up leave or PTO. I lasted two weeks before I returned. It was too soon, but I didn't know what else to do with myself. Battling with insurance companies and financial institutions had taken its toll and I needed to get out of the house.

Up until March, I'd been splitting my week between our company warehouse in Berkeley and our main office in San Francisco. San Francisco is one of my favorite cities and I never tired of exiting the BART every morning. I loved the art and architecture everywhere I looked. But the San Francisco office had an open floor plan with no privacy. The thought of going back to that when everyone knew that Bill had just died was too much to bear. I couldn't handle people coming up to me to offer condolences.

However, the customer service team was based in the Berkeley warehouse. It was a small group, all women, and I knew them much better than I did those in San Francisco. I also had my own office in Berkeley.

My first day back was brutal. My boss came in to see me and said "Jamie... I'm just so so sorry...," and I lost it. He looked so heartbroken for me that I couldn't take it. The director of Human Resources also came in and asked if I was ready to return. I said "Honestly, I don't know what else to do!" I spent most of the day running to the bathroom where I could close a stall door and cry.

About a week later, I got up the nerve to return to San Francisco. The BART ride there was 45 minutes, which meant being stuck with my own thoughts for 45 minutes twice per day. The city I once loved so much now seemed harsh because every step reminded me of somewhere Bill and I had explored.

Our company celebrates all birthdays on the first of the month and mine, unfortunately, is in April. This meant celebrating with the office three weeks after my husband died. Around noon that day, an email went around saying we'd gather in the kitchen in two hours. I was seized by pure panic. I closed my laptop, stuffed it in my backpack, and went to the elevator. I ran all the way to the BART station and gasped for air on the platform. It took the entire ride home to calm down enough to just be able to breathe.

☼

Becky was also struggling. She had worked for Bill back in New York and he jokingly called her the son he never had. She's twelve years younger than I am and earned the nickname Junior because we're so similar. Bill and Junior had had a hilarious relationship, behaving like teenage boys together. She missed him profoundly. As she often pointed out, she felt he was one of the few men who wasn't a complete asshole.

One night, Junior texted me to say she hadn't heard from Bill lately. He'd been visiting us in our sleep, visits where the sensations were far too strong to just be dreams.

That night, Junior asked, "Where has he gone?" I sat with it for a while because I didn't know. I felt the same way and didn't understand it. Junior and I joked that he was traveling the Universe, listening to the Grateful Dead and riding a cosmic wave. But to hear nothing from him compounded my grief.

I slept fitfully. At one point, I looked at the time. It was around 4 am. I tried to go back to sleep and as I did, I thought "say hi to Junior when you can." I fell asleep hard - one of those deep, black sleeps that often elude me.

At 8, I woke up to series of texts from Junior. She had woken up scared and confused and happy all at the same time, convinced Bill had visited her. I looked at the time stamp on her texts; they were from 5 am.

07

Bill was a chef by trade and had taught in two culinary programs back in New York before we moved to California. He had amazing relationships with many of his students. Since Bill was an adult learner when he went to culinary school, I felt it would be fitting to set up a culinary scholarship in his honor.

I asked our friends back in New York for help and was put in touch with one of the heads at the Buffalo chapter of the American Culinary Foundation. She assured me that we could set up a fund that could be used at both programs in the area. She told me that if we were able to get the scholarship over a certain amount, it would become an endowment and we would be able to provide assistance to students every year. My only stipulation was that I wanted it to go to a returning student in need, like Bill had been.

We set up a GoFundMe campaign and arranged a fundraiser lunch in Buffalo for the first weekend in May. The lunch was to be held at one of Bill's favorite restaurants and the chef-owner was one of the kindest souls in the restaurant scene there.

I threw myself into a frenzy over the scholarship. I felt so strongly that something positive had to come from losing him. By the time the lunch rolled around, we'd raised enough money to astonish the organizer. After everything was tallied, she emailed me *"This is so wonderful! It often takes years to make the endowment value progress that has been put together so quickly in your husband's name. This action on your part will be impacting students and the culinary field for generations."* People had accomplished this out of love for Bill and their bond with him over their love of hospitality.

April was not done with me by any stretch of the imagination. In the middle of the month Klaus and I were up at the house when I woke up one morning to find that he'd been sick on the couch. This was unusual for him. He had a stomach of steel and never sullied the furniture. He didn't want to eat, either. Worried, I called around. No local vets had available appointments because it was a Sunday. By mid-morning, he had lain back down and was increasingly lethargic. I panicked. I packed him up and we drove back down to Oakland because I knew we'd have a better shot at finding an emergency clinic there.

The entire drive down, my brain screamed. I was too scared to cry. I silently begged Klaus to make it. He was all I had left and I couldn't lose him too – I just couldn't.

We finally made it to Oakland and I helped him out of the car. He immediately threw up again. I began to cry but had to pull myself together to help him. We didn't even bother going into the house – I looked up an emergency clinic in the area and we went straight there.

Klaus was too sick to be frightened. He curled up in my arms in the examination room. The vet tech walked through my options and warned me how much it would cost. "Anything," I said.

They took Klaus in the back and asked me to wait. For three hours, I waited and couldn't breathe.

The vet tech finally brought him around and told me the good news: they couldn't find anything wrong. His blood work looked good, his x-rays looked good. It was probably something he ate. I began to cry again, this time out of relief. We paid the bill – I didn't even think to ask how much it was – and we went home.

The next morning was cold and gray and rainy. I watched in dull horror as Notre Dame de Paris burned down, and I turned 45.

The fundraising lunch in Buffalo was in May, and I faced the trip with excitement but deep reservations. I was looking forward to seeing my friends, but I was still too tender to be around a lot of people. There was the additional bitter pill of going alone when Bill and I had originally planned to go to Buffalo together.

About a year before Bill died, an acquaintance had asked me if I would be interested in submitting some poems to be considered for a show. The concept was called "The Art of Words" and artists would visually interpret the accepted pieces, and then the art and poetry would be displayed together. I loved the idea. I had never written poetry before but I decided to give it a go. I nervously submitted two poems. To my shock, both were accepted. Bill and I decided to go to the opening and see how the artists interpreted my work. In true Bill fashion, he turned the trip into an adventure by suggesting we drive cross-country for it.

Now that Bill was gone, I decided to combine the trip with the fundraiser luncheon. After our lovely meal with friends and family, we went to the opening. It was interesting to see my words on the wall and to meet some of the authors and artists. I don't consider myself a writer; I just managed to get some words that resonated with other people down on paper. Regardless, it felt so good to be there, with my friends, surrounded by words and images.

The next day, I met my former student Jim for lunch. It feels odd to call him my student, because he's a Franciscan brother in his 60s. I had met him a few years earlier when he applied to an English as a Second Language (ESL) graduate program I was running. He had wanted to talk to me before enrolling because he was worried that he'd been out of school for too long. He'd spent time in Italy and understood what it was like to live somewhere where the language was not his own. I told him this would be a strength if he became an ESL teacher. After talking with him for about an hour, I was confident that he would not only do well but also bring something special to our classes. And he did. He was one of the best students I ever worked with.

After moving to California, Jim and I stayed in touch. He began to refer to himself as my stalker and kept trying to lure me back to Buffalo. He was a sweet and kind soul and an email from him always brightened my day.

When I told Jim that Bill had died, I knew it would devastate him. Meeting up with him in Buffalo was hard. His face was pale and drawn, as if he'd been crying all night. Just seeing him made me want to breakdown again too. I stared down at my tea a lot, trying to hold it together.

By the time I flew back to Oakland, I was more than ready to try to return to normal. I was so tired of being on the receiving end of sympathetic looks, even though I knew they were out of love. I also felt that I couldn't open up and laugh around our Buffalo family. I felt like everyone was expecting me to be openly weeping all the time. But it is possible to be completely heartbroken and still recognize the absurdity of life, and I was exhausted from having to pretend otherwise.

08

My friend Claudia was a huge comfort during the dark days of that spring. Since her brother Matt had died two days before Bill, we were both experiencing similar rollercoaster rides of emotion. For me, it always happened that just when I thought "I seem to be ok today...", I'd break down again. It was unpredictable and overwhelming and she got it because she was right there in it too.

Claudia and I had known each other since kindergarten. We were in different crowds in high school but it never mattered. We always found each other hilarious. After high school we'd kept in touch but hadn't actually seen each other in about 16 years.

But that spring, the stress of her life started causing her to fantasize about getting away for a bit. She asked if she could come visit me in Lake County. She loved wine, so I planned and re-planned wine tasting trips and we decided she'd visit in September. Her trip gave me something to look forward to when there seemed to be nothing else.

During my drives back and forth between Oakland and Lake County, I had a lot of time to think. Bill and I had wanted to set up classes for wine tasting or cooking out of the house because we loved Lake County and wanted to support local wineries. Napa sources a lot of grapes from Lake County and we felt it was only a matter of time before the area got the recognition it deserved. I still wanted to plug into the scene so I kept mulling over ways to do so. I visited a few wineries and introduced myself, volunteering to help if any was needed. I'm sure they all thought I was crazy – like, why is this woman offering to work for free?

Eventually I found the Lake County Wine Council and emailed them. Within the week, the director called me. We chatted for a few minutes before I spilled that my husband had just died and I was trying to make a life for myself in Lake County. She assured me that it was a wonderful community and I'd be in good hands, then asked if I wanted to help with an event over the summer. I jumped at the opportunity.

About a week later, she emailed me. She told me that she had reviewed my credentials and realized I might instead want to be a judge for the Lake County Wines competition.

Hell. Yeah.

I was bursting with excitement. The director asked if I knew anyone else who might be able to do it. I thought of Bridget. She'd been in the wine industry for over 20 years and had just passed her Certified Wine

Specialist exam. And I wanted to work a wine event with one of my favorite people. Before we knew it, it was all booked and Bridget would be joining me in Lake County in June.

It was starting to feel like it might be possible to survive.

09

Bill and I never made New Year's resolutions. Instead, we made a list of goals to focus on in the coming year. On January 1, 2019, we took a long walk around Lake Chabot and talked excitedly about all of the changes we wanted to make to our new house. As soon as we got back to the cottage, we made our list of home improvements. Bill hung it on the side of the refrigerator.

I used this list as my plan of attack. I'd never been a homeowner before and hesitated over what to do first. I went with the biggest: replacing the roof. We had known we would need a new roof when we bought it, and the rains of the past winter had only made the situation worse. I knew Bill had investigated a few roofing companies so I went into his email, found a quote, and contacted the company.

Next was installing an HVAC system. The house was originally a vacation cottage, so instead of heat it only had a fireplace. Our real estate agent put me in touch with a fantastic company, and it turned out that Bill had already talked to them. The workers were incredibly kind when I told them he had passed.

One by one, I checked off our list. My brother came to visit and he helped me repaint some rooms and plant a lemon tree and an olive tree.

I tore out the awful carpet in one bedroom and hired a neighbor to install laminate. I was proud of taking the reins on the house. It was slowly shifting from "ours" to "mine."

It was time to talk to my boss about going remote so I could finally move in full time and make it my home.

Sorting out the finances took months. It took many, many phone calls and more patience than I knew I had. Several accounts told me he was the one that needed to call and I would always ask how they advised I make that happen. Others were more helpful and one even sent a grief care package to me. But through all of the muck, I came to realize that it was incredibly empowering to be in charge of my own financial future.

This was a first for me. Bill was twenty years my senior. Although I had come into the relationship with a well-padded retirement account of my own, he had been working through his portfolio for much longer. Figuring that he knew what he was doing, I handed everything over to him.

It was harrowing, once he was gone, to have no idea if I had any money other than my 401k, let alone the rights to my home. Once I sorted everything out, I swore I would never again allow myself that level of ignorance and confusion. If I had to be in control, I would kick ass at it.

There were no excuses for otherwise.

Every Saturday, one of our favorite Lake County wineries hosted a farmer's market. I decided to check it out one rainy June morning. It was fairly bleak, so early in the season, but I met a caterer I had chatted with on social media and then checked out some vendors. Bill was so passionate about supporting local farmers that I felt it would be a good place to start meeting people.

One of the vendors was selling small stained-glass ornaments. They were stunning and I picked up one with veins of blue running through it. It was about the size of my hand and caught the light beautifully. The vendor began telling me about how color therapy works and it would change my aura. I nodded, pretending to listen, but I was thinking "Ok, chick, whatever..." I stopped myself because the one thing I've learned after losing Bill is that I don't know shit about the universe. Maybe she was right. I bought it.

I was getting ready to leave the market when another vendor caught my eye. She was selling jewelry made of stones and gems wrapped in cut brass. I noticed one necklace in particular, a flat piece of red-brown variegated stone with a metal casing that was cut to look like a mountainscape with the sun above it. Something about it drew me in. I picked it up and it felt like all of Lake County was encapsulated in that pendant – I felt the heat of the sun just looking at it. The artist said to me "By the way, that's called wonderstone." I froze. "What did you just say?" She looked surprised. "That stone – it's called wonderstone." Done. I bought it.

She had no way of knowing that it was what we called the house. Bill and I originally called it Wonderland because there were so many surprises tucked into nooks and crannies around the yard. But we both loved dumb movies, especially the movie The Incredible Burt Wonderstone, so we started calling the house Wonderstone as a tribute to the film and the name stuck.

It turns out that wonderstone is a type of jasper found around volcanic areas, including Mount Konocti in Lake County. It's believed to promote overall wellbeing. For me, it was a posthumous gift from Bill and I wore it with the necklace that held his ashes. On particularly rough days I gripped the two to help me through and they always did.

Although I was beginning to feel like I had a plan developing for the house and, by extension, for my life, I was lonely as hell. Klaus and I were constant motion between Oakland and Lake County, so I didn't have me to connect with anyone in either place. By June, I began reaching out o friends and inviting them to visit.

I sent a message to an acquaintance named Eric who I knew through he wine industry in Santa Ynez Valley. He'd left his job a year before nd had been travelling around the country with his dog. Bill and I had dmired his resolve and dreamed of doing the same with Klaus.

"Hey," I began. "No idea where you are these days but if you find ourself in Northern California and need somewhere to land for a bit, let e know! You're welcome to my place, whether I'm there or not."

A few moments later, Eric replied "Holy shit! You're not going to elieve this, but I was just about to message you to see how you were."

Bill and I knew Eric from visiting his winery. We were living in Long each at the time and had gone up to Santa Ynez for a long weekend. Our first stop was at Zaca Mesa because we loved the Rhône style wines roduced there. We chatted with the woman pouring in the tasting room nd when we said we were from Long Beach, she said "Oh, our winemaker sed to live there! Let me get him!" Eric appeared and talked shop with us r a few minutes before offering us a quick tour. He gave us his business ard before we left and we stayed in touch via social media.

A few months later, Bill and I moved to Solvang, where I worked as a sommelier in a restaurant. One of the first local winemakers that we featured was Eric. My boss asked me to do a write up on him for our website, so I reached out with a few questions. He was friendly enough but kept professional distance. That was fine with me; I also tended to keep a hard line between my professional and private life.

Later that month he came to the café to pour during happy hour. He looked miserable, which made me laugh because I usually felt the same way. I made small talk with him between customers, mostly about our dogs.

Those were the extent of my physical interactions with Eric. When he left his job and traveled around the country, I sent him a few messages to cheer him on because I thought it was totally badass. Who drops out of life in their mid-40s to travel? Not many, and Bill and I were envious.

But things were different when I reached out in June. We began texting throughout the day. I was amazed at how much we had in common. Countless times, I'd say something and he'd reply "I was just about to say the same thing!" It felt like we'd know each other forever. He cheered me up during a very dark time.

And then one evening, he texted "Hey, can we talk? I can't text this ast!" I froze. Did I want to talk to him? Did he think I was interested in something more than a friendship? I didn't want to give him the wrong mpression. I stared at my phone for a few minutes and then thought "Why not?"

We ended up talking for an hour, something I hadn't done in years. I 'elt drained when we finally hung up.

10

By June, I was also already beginning to dread the holidays. Thanksgiving was such a Bill holiday and he'd always spent weeks planning and replanning our dinner. The year before, we'd had it at our home in Lake County for the first time and the thought of being there with only Klaus was too much.

Out of the blue, my friend Manu asked if he'd be able to visit me. He lives in Paris and we'd been friends for well over a decade. I'd visited him many times in Paris.

Since Manu wasn't American, Thanksgiving didn't hold any special meaning for him. A visit from him around then felt like the perfect antidote to holiday blues. I jumped at the opportunity and asked him to book his tickets as soon as possible.

Bridget arrived mid-June. I had been so excited to see her again and to experience the wine competition together. But it happened that the competition was held the same week as my mother's open-heart surgery. I never would have accepted, but her surgery was rescheduled three times and after changing plane tickets and hotel reservations each time, my brother assured me he'd be with her so I didn't need to be.

I was on edge the entire competition. I'd be as professional as possible during the tasting and then check my phone constantly for updates.

I was also worried about Klaus. He wasn't the same without Bill. He used to watch the door for Bill to come home from work, but hadn't since March. He was still playful and loving, but he'd curl up in his bed alone some nights and not want to sleep with me. He was just as heartbroken as I was. Although Aaron said he would watch him while I was at the competition, worried about leaving him without anyone from his pack.

By the last day, I was drained. It was an invaluable experience, but wasn't in the shape to be around people for so long. My brother texted me that evening to say that our mom had come out of the surgery and everything looked fine. I almost wept with relief.

The next week, I got approval to work remotely full time and I faced the task of packing up all of my stuff and moving to Lake County permanently.

※

During my marriage to Bill, I'd gained some weight. He never mentioned it, but the extra 15 pounds were obvious on my frame and I felt bloated and tired most of the time.

After he died, I was hit with a wave of nausea alongside the grief. Once I was able to think more clearly, I understood that I had to be my healthiest self if I wanted to survive. I focused on clean eating, yoga, and hiking. I swam at the pool and even went running at the gym - and I hate running. By July, I'd dropped seventeen pounds and felt physically better than I had in years.

Yoga helped me tremendously. I'd been into yoga on and off for years and I felt like it would be good to get on the mat. In the first few months, though, it just was not possible. The thought of being stuck in my mind during class was too brutal.

But once I could go, it was beautiful. Yoga slowly and steadily opened me up again. I was gentle with myself and if something didn't feel right, I didn't do it. If I cried, I cried. I let my body be. These were some of the only moments in which I wasn't worrying about the future. I allowed the sorrow to wash over me and once I did, it would dissipate.

As I prepared to live at the house full time, there were still countless little tweaks I needed to make. I dreaded going to the hardware store after an ill-fated trip for paint to redo the bathroom.

The young woman working the paint department asked me "Do you need matte or glossy?" I had no idea. What the fuck did I need? Why were there so many choices to make? Couldn't I just order paint and get some fucking paint?

Why did EVERYTHING have to turn into an ordeal that I was in no shape to handle?

"I have no idea what I'm doing," I told her. Her eyes grew big and she handed me a sheet of info about types of paint. I didn't read it. I just ordered an enormous tub of white paint and got out of there as quickly as could. I'm sure at least half of that tub is still at the house, untouched.

A few weeks later, I had to go back for outlet covers. I knew what needed and I knew where to find it, so I figured I could avoid human contact I almost made it out in one piece, until the cashier struck up a conversation

"What's that? An acorn?"

I realized she was looking at my necklace.

"Yeah, sort of..." I replied.

She asked, "Is it like a locket?"

"Yes..." and I went for broke, "It has some of my husband's ashes in it."

The woman didn't look surprised. She didn't look sad. She didn't lowe her eyes and mumble "I'm so sorry" like everyone else. Instead, she smile brightly and said "That's beautiful! I hope my kids do that for me!"

I found myself continuing to talk, unable to stop. There was finall someone who didn't greet what was going on with judgement of any kind not even pity. "The rest of his ashes are at the base of our pear trees. H planted them for our anniversary a few months ago." She beamed and replied, "And he's making sure you have beautiful fruit!"

When I taught ESL, my older students always told me they thought it was weird that Americans ask "How are you?" when we don't want to know. They have a point -- It's a strange custom. We ask, but any answer other than "Fine!" isn't acceptable. We're more focused on people pretending to be ok than we are on how they actually feel.

In the same way, the window of time we provide to people who are grieving is outrageously short. I admittedly returned to work too soon, so maybe that gave the false impression that I was "fine." (I fucking hate that word.) Still, I was shocked when a colleague expressed surprise that I was "still so sad" two months after Bill had died.

The cashier was such a stellar example of how to interact with everyone. She saw the beauty in what had happened, not the sadness. She handled me with grace, and it was something I needed to learn to do for myself.

11

By July, Eric and I were chatting for hours a couple of times per week. Some nights I was a total mess and would say so. He never tried to cheer me up or give me the "Oh, you'll be fine!" bullshit. He'd reply that he was sorry, that he couldn't imagine how I was feeling, and to let him know if there's anything he could do.

It helped that Eric had known Bill as a living, breathing person.

As my move to Lake County approached, Eric offered to help. I thought he was out of his mind. I was three hours north of him already and about to move even further. Did he really want to spend a weekend helping an acquaintance move five hours away? He insisted he did, and said that I shouldn't waste money on a moving crew when we could do it. I skeptically agreed.

As July drew to a close, I spent more time down in Oakland to finish packing up the cottage. I'd made less progress than expected because I was so drained. Packing Bill's belongings without him slowed me down. A lot. I did what I could, but more often than not, I'd collapse on the couch and watch Broad City to laugh away my woes.

After so much contact, Eric unexpectedly went silent a few weeks before the move. Nothing. I knew something was up and sure enough, he posted pictures from San Francisco on social media. He didn't owe me anything, but I was hurt that he hadn't mentioned he would be in the Bay Area. It seemed so strange to me.

As we got closer to the move, I was convinced that he was going to cancel. I began to resent my reliance on him. We had about two weeks until the move and I hadn't heard from him in several days. I texted "I know you're really busy so if you have too much going on, I totally understand. Just let me know either way because I don't have much time to book movers."

He replied immediately. "I'm still coming! I wouldn't let ya down."

His change from "you" to the more indirect, casual "ya" was telling.

Still, I reasoned, I was happy to have his help. We were, in my mind, friends. Maybe I'd read all of his texts and calls wrong, and he was someone who got close to other people and then ghosted. I told myself that it was fine if that was the case; I had no emotional energy to spare.

The day Eric arrived, I still had a lot to do. I felt badly that I wasn't better prepared, and annoyed that he was in my space. Why was he here in my home with Bill? It felt like such an intrusion, even though I knew I had been looking forward to it.

Klaus was also not having it. He growled constantly at both Eric and Eric's dog Ichi. They ended up in our office space to try to give Klaus time to

alm down. I'm sure Eric had noticed the energy shift, because the first day
was beyond awkward. All of those easy phone conversations evaporated
nd I struggled to even be polite.

Luckily for all, The Muppets came to our rescue. It was the 40th
nniversary of *The Muppet Movie* and it was playing in theaters for one
ight only. I love the Muppets and had to go. Eric had said he wanted to as
well, so I'd gotten tickets in advance.

We took a taxi to the theater and Eric smuggled in a bottle of gamay.
he seats began to fill up and I cracked up to see that a lot of people had
ome in costume. Who knew that was a thing? People were all decked out
s their Muppet alter egos. I dug it.

We settled in to watch the movie, sipping the gamay. I sang out loud to
very song and Eric kept laughing at my enthusiasm. He told me later that
 was the first time he'd ever seen me so happy and he loved the joy on
y face.

By the time we got back to the cottage, the energy between us had
hifted. We chatted away, and he said he was stunned by how deep The
Muppets got. Eventually we called it a night because we wanted to get an
arly start the next morning.

The next day we packed up the UHaul. Eric drove it up the day after and I followed in my Jeep with Klaus. On the other end, Aaron helped unload. By July 28th we were all done and Lake County was my home.

12

August was brutally hot and I fantasized about escaping to Northern California. I found a cottage on the coast in Mendocino County and booked it to coincide with the full moon. As it drew near, I had a bad feeling about it. I couldn't articulate why I felt so unsettled and disturbed, but I knew I had to cancel.

On August 12, I got an email from my doctor that I needed a follow-up on a recent mammogram. I called the doctor's office. "She said she needs to see you immediately," said the receptionist. "Can you tell me why?" I asked. "No - no other information. Just that you need to come back immediately."

Well *fuck*.

I booked an appointment and drove back down to Oakland. I was a nervous wreck the entire way. My biggest fear when Bill was alive had been that I would get cancer and he'd have to go through the stress of losing another spouse.

The day was spent being ushered from one room to another. The first technician had a terrible bedside manner. She barked orders at me and chided me for moving during the mammogram. "I told you to stand still!" she said. I was near tears and could only reply "I thought I was."

I went to another room and waited some more. A follow up sonogram had been ordered because of a worrisome mass in the imaging. The second technician was very kind. She had me wait a little more and then came back with "I have good news – you're fine." I slumped with relief and she said "Oh honey, I saw your chart – I saw what you've been through this year. I hope this is a little less worry for you now."

By the time I got to back to my car, I was exhausted. Bridget had texted me to see how it went and I noticed the date: August 15th. August 15th. Why did that seem so familiar, I wondered? And then I remembered: I was supposed to be in Mendocino at the coastal cottage. This was why I had to cancel.

And that's how August continued. I fought and fought to pull myself out of the pit and build my life back up. Eric and I were talking all of the time by then and we began to make plans to see one another. Any of the initial tension from the move had long since dissipated and it felt like we'd known each other forever. Maybe we can thank The Muppets for that.

He said I was his best friend and I felt similarly. We told each other everything and I never held back about the pain of losing Bill. I wasn't ready to start seeing anyone romantically, but it felt so good to be able to trust someone and confide in him. He never asked anything in return.

Eric bought us October tickets to the opera in San Francisco. I figured that no matter what we "were" by then, we would have a great weekend together. October was two months away and Eric was heading into harvest, so we knew we wouldn't be able to get together in September. We agreed that Labor Day weekend would be the last chance to see each other, and I offered to come down to Paso Robles. It was a five-hour drive, but I wanted to see other friends in the Central Coast while I was down there. On top of that, working remotely meant my schedule was flexible.

I asked Aaron if he could watch Klaus for the weekend. He agreed, but something wasn't sitting right with me. About a week before I was supposed to head south, I had the same feeling of dread that I'd had in August. I called Junior to see if she could watch Klaus that weekend. "I'm sorry, I can't – we're having work done, so it's too loud here. Why can't Aaron watch him?" I explained that he could but that something was telling me it was a bad idea. "Aaron takes good care of him, right?" she asked. Of course. Aaron loved him almost as much as I did. It wasn't Aaron that I was worried about, but I couldn't articulate what it was. I just knew something would happen.

And then it did.

13

The Thursday before Labor Day, I was excited as I packed for my trip. I was going to San Francisco first for some work meetings and then I'd head to Paso from there. I kept squeezing Klaus, feeling badly that I'd be away from him and trying to talk myself into believing that he'd be fine. But still, my dread grew by the hour.

I still don't know how it happened. The yard was completely fenced and none of the gates were open. He was outside for five minutes. When he didn't scratch at the door to be let back in, I went out to look for him. I checked all of his usual spots; he was nowhere to be seen. I'd usually hear him rustling around somewhere if he was into something, but the yard was eerily silent.

And then I saw his little body across the street, stone still, and I knew.

I ran out and collapsed next to him. A car had hit him; there was blood pouring from his nose and mouth. I couldn't lose him too, it couldn't happen. But he was gone. I picked up his body and squeezed him, screaming at the top of my lungs. His blood was all over me but I didn't care.

I brought his body to a high spot in our yard and sat with him for a long time. I kept kissing him and apologizing to him and to Bill. How could this have happened? How could they BOTH be gone? How could they BOTH have died at the place we loved so much?

Aaron came out to talk to me, looking stunned, but I waved him away. I couldn't talk. I was beyond words. My boy was gone.

Aaron dug a grave between the pear trees. I called my mom and Bridget and told them what had happened. I also called Eric and told him I wasn't coming down. I couldn't move. I sat with Klaus's body on my lap. I couldn't put this beautiful boy in the ground.

Eventually, Aaron told me he was ready. I wrapped Klaus in a quilt he had loved. I wanted to curl up in the grave myself and just have it over with. This was too much to take.

I laid Klaus in the grave and couldn't say anything. Aaron might have, I don't remember. I ran into the house and took the rest of Bill's ashes off of the altar I'd made for him on my dresser. I poured all of them in with Klaus. At least they'd be together.

After we finished burying Klaus, I turned to go back to the house. I knew, suddenly, that I couldn't spend another night there. Both Bill and Klaus died there and I had to get as far away as I could. I asked Eric if I could come down after all and he said "Please do. Stay as long as you need to."

I went inside, washed Klaus's blood off of me, changed my clothes, and told Aaron I was leaving. He asked, "Where are you going?" I said Paso for now. I don't know after that." And then he said, "What if there's an emergency?" I asked "Like what?"

What could possibly be an emergency? The worst had happened.

ash

/aSH/
plural noun: ashes
1. the powdery residue left after the burning
   of a substance.
- the remains of something destroyed; ruins.
   *"the people are really living in the ashes of those
   traditions and institutions"*
- the remains of the human body after cremation
   or burning.
   "his ashes were scattered on a Welsh mountainside"
- powdery material thrown out by a volcano.
   "the plains have been showered by volcanic ash"
- the mineral component of an organic substance, as
   assessed from the residue left after burning.
   *"coal contains higher levels of ash than
   premium fuels"*

Ashes to ashes, dust to dust

Rising from the ashes

14

I don't remember most of the drive to Paso Robles that night. I just remember reaching over to pet Klaus and realizing that he wasn't there.

September was a lost month. I drifted between hotels and rented rooms around Sonoma County as I tried to make sense of what had happened. I only went to the house to pack, always getting out as quickly as possible. The weight of losing my family crushed me and I didn't think I would survive. I would pray at night to not wake up in the morning because I didn't believe I had the strength to live anymore.

Nothing made sense. Everything I'd worked towards was gone. My little family unit, my home, the new routines I'd made with Klaus, the social connections I'd made - they were all gone. It felt like the past six months had been pointless. I took a leave from work - I couldn't remember where I was half the time, let alone keep track of work demands - so the structure of a daily job was also gone. Everything around which I'd built my identity vanished, just like that.

※

Whenever I was in Paso I would stay at Eric's place. While he went to work, I spent hours weeping, unable to stop. I would drive into Paso Robles or San Luis Obispo on occasion, but I was often too exhausted to do anything once I got there. I tried going on long drives to clear my mind but it didn't work.

Eric constantly brought home groceries he thought I might like, but I couldn't eat much. He assured me that I was no bother, but I felt like I shouldn't be around him for too long. I couldn't even make conversation.

I contacted Manu immediately to make sure he hadn't bought a plane ticket to visit me for Thanksgiving. He hadn't, but he suggested that I visit him instead. I booked a flight to Paris that same day. I didn't have to run the trip by anyone; I didn't have to make plans for Klaus. It hit me hard that I was totally alone.

※

By mid-September I got an Airbnb in Santa Rosa for a week. It was within striking distance of the house and I began to pack up everything that I had spent the previous four weeks unpacking. I tried not to think about how I'd only lived in the house for a month; the thought would inevitably spin me out again.

Every time I went to the house, my brain screamed in pain. The stress of being there brought on raging headaches, which made the task of packing up even more brutal.

I'd heard about brain fog that widows experience, but whatever I'd had after Bill died was nothing compared to this double hit. I would lose track of conversations halfway through. Sometimes I would come to while driving and have no idea where I was supposed to be going. It started to frighten me, but I was helpless to stop it.

Life around me didn't stop just because mine felt like it was over. I had to make decisions about where I would live. Our real estate agent very gently talked me through the paperwork to get the house listed. I was fine answering legal questions about whether anyone had died on the property, but I'd lose it when I had to talk about the improvements I'd made. I'd put so much blood, sweat, and tears into it with the hopes of seeing our vision through. It all seemed completely futile.

I had deleted my social media accounts the night Klaus was killed. I couldn't fathom having to have all of those conversations again, or worse, people telling me that Klaus was "just a dog." I asked Bridget to tell the friends who would care that I wasn't up for talking.

However, our real estate agent asked me to go back on social media so I could share the listing and I begrudgingly did. I wanted to be rid of the house as soon as possible. Two weeks after Klaus was killed I logged back in to Facebook and posted this:

I wasn't going to post this but I realize it's worse having to explain
over and over to people individually - so off comes the tourniquet.

On August 28th, Klaus got out of the yard at the house and was killed
I don't know how he got out but it doesn't matter. I found his body acros
the street and I just snapped.

He's buried in the yard between the pear trees that Bill had plante
for our anniversary. I left that night and have only been back for a fe
hours to pack.

This is why I am selling the house. Believe me - I have no desire c
energy to move yet again. But I absolutely cannot stay in the place that m
family died within six months of each other. We'd bought that place wit
such joy and promise and now to be there alone with both of them gon
is just too much.

I don't know where I'll land, so please do not ask me where I'r
moving. I really don't know. I've been bouncing around between Sonom
and the Central Coast. I've taken leave from work because bickering wit
strangers about promo codes is the absolute last thing I give a fuck abou
(Work has, yet again, been beyond helpful and understanding.) I will b
out of the country for Thanksgiving because I can't bear the though
of being here without them, and will likely do the same for Christma

It seemed like a brilliant idea to get married on December 28th... now, not so much...)

No, I'm not ok so please do not ask if I am. I'm really not up for another round of public "I'm so sorry!" but I also am not up for the conversations. I am not up to talk about it all and thank you for understanding that.

Many people called immediately. I knew it was out of concern, so I answered when I could. I had learned from losing Bill that trying to reply to everyone was the opposite of self-care, especially if it meant replying to people who otherwise never reached out.

At some point, I found myself at the beach in Santa Cruz. I don't remember why I went. I parked and walked over to the pier. It was crowded, so it must have been a weekend. There were some standard beach-town tchotchke shops selling t-shirts and keychains. I walked out onto the pier, trying to hold it together in public but failing miserably. Tears were streaming down my face. I kept my sunglasses on and kept walking. The sun and sea air felt good. I kept my head down and hoped no one would stop to ask if I was okay. No one did.

I walked over to the rail to watch the waves for a few minutes. Down below was a landing with some sea lions soaking up the sun. I stared down and thought "I miss my pack."

Santa Cruz felt suddenly pointless, and I turned to leave. As I walked along the sidewalk, I noticed a vendor selling silver jewelry. I stopped to look at rings and he began asking me standard tourist bait questions. "Where are you visiting from?" he asked. I replied "I'm not really sure" because I didn't know how to answer. I had no permanent address. "You don't know where you live?" I didn't answer.

I picked up a ring of a crescent moon and a little star. I didn't even really want it but I asked how much it was. He named a price and I handed him the cash and left.

I walked back to my car and saw that I had a parking ticket. I didn't care. I tossed it onto the passenger's seat and then broke down crying again because Klaus should have been on the seat instead.

I got into my car and drove off again, not clear on where I was going.

As I struggled with the grief of losing Klaus, my body reacted accordingly. I began getting my period every two weeks. At first, I worried that something was wrong. I'd just gotten my annual checkup a few weeks before Klaus was killed. Everything was fine as far as the doctor was concerned. But still, I worried. It happened again, and I realized that my body was trying to purge all of the toxic trauma.

This certainly isn't unique to my experience. A friend who also lost her husband suddenly experienced extreme fatigue about two years later. Even though she was a fitness coach, she suddenly felt like she couldn't get out of bed. She thought she was coming down with something. We talked through what was going on and she revealed that her son had been arrested. She was living alone for the first time since her husband had died. I asked her if her body could be conserving energy so she'd be able to process all of the emotions she was experiencing. She was silent for a moment and then said "Yes, that's absolutely what's happening."

For the rest of the month, my mind was consumed with the logistics of the move. Eric had helped last time, but now he was in the thick of harvest and wouldn't be able to drive up to Lake County again. Besides, he'd done more than enough to help me already. I thought about attempting it on my own, but the thought of piecing it all together when I'd just done it a month before was too overwhelming. I gave in and hired a moving crew to handle everything.

In the meantime, I found a rental in Cambria along the Central Coast. It was about 45 minutes away from Eric. I worried that I was clinging to him too much, so having a reasonable distance between us seemed like a good idea. I liked Cambria and the apartment was three blocks from the ocean. I could sit on a bench, breathing in the ocean air, and let the grief consume me. Bill had loved the Pacific Ocean. It struck me as incredibly cruel that he wasn't with me to see it.

15

I was due to be in New York in October, so I decided to move everything out of the house before I left. The moving crew and I negotiated dates back and forth but the only date they had available was September 28th, which was Bill's birthday.

Despite all that had happened, this was the worst pain of all. I spent September 27th packing. The emotional pain was so severe, I felt myself squinting the entire time. My skull felt like it was splitting in half.

The day of the move was predictably brutal, but the movers were considerate. They brought me flowers and donuts. I rarely eat fast food but donuts seemed appropriate. I grabbed a bottle of very expensive wine and drank it alone that night. We would drive down to Cambria the next morning.

The move was over by September 30th and I unpacked everything in my little place. The rest of our stuff was in a local storage unit. I did some laundry and packed back up because I had to fly to New York the next day.

The October trip to New York was originally supposed to be a work trip. I was going to spend a few days working a trade show in the city and visiting some friends, and the rest of the week would be out on Long Island at my mother's.

Even though I was on leave from work, I had still planned to attend the event in New York. However, I soon realized it would be emotional hell to see my colleagues. I asked if someone else could work it. Ever the optimist, I still wanted to see some of my favorite coworkers and I made plans to get together with them for dinner.

The trip arrived. I had every day scheduled, with places I was supposed to be all over Long Island and New York City. But as soon as I got to my mom's house, my brain froze at the thought of spending the week taking trains, taxis, and subways back and forth.

I cancelled everything and on everyone and crawled into bed at my mom's. I did nothing that week except eat bagels and sleep. It was exactly what I needed. I had worried so much about letting people down that I wasn't giving myself any space to rest and recover.

I also noticed who offered to come visit me. It was refreshing to know who would show up and who wouldn't. I felt like I understood where to invest my emotional energy, and that alone was priceless.

After I landed back in California, I had to figure out what to do with myself. My life was blasted wide open and I had no goals or plans of my own. After so much loss, my body and soul were begging for relief and I knew I had to focus on healthier ways to make that happen.

October was spent outside. I hiked down to the water, around Fiscalini Ranch, over to Harmony Headlands, and up in San Simeon. I walked down to town and around Moonstone Beach. I joined a hiking club and walked to the Cambria Cemetery with them on Halloween. I was studying Spanish, reading, and writing outside, too. The sunshine was soothing and I loved watching the different birds have turf wars with each other.

I unpacked everything and set up my new place. It came together quickly because it was so small. I enjoyed the cozy living room and office space. I left the bedroom window open every night to hear the ocean crashing and owls hooting. I loved it but it all felt so fleeting. I'd gone from Oakland to Lake County to Cambria in less than two months, and then left for New York immediately after the move. Soon Eric and I would be going to San Francisco for the weekend, and then I'd leave for Europe only days after that. I began to wonder why I was attempting to find a home when my life was going in so many directions at once.

Eric came over every weekend for dinner or a hike. Between visits, I enjoyed having the whole week to myself. Although I loved spending time with him, a niggling part of my brain worried that we were together for the wrong reasons. Was I just clinging to him because he was so steady through all of my turbulence? My gut told me he was solid but my mind was just too muddled.

I thought a lot about when Bill and I had begun dating. It was about two and a half years after his wife Laura had died and Bill still saw many of her friends and colleagues on a regular basis. Early on, several of them told me that I was "nothing like" Laura. I still don't know whether this was meant as a compliment or not. Either way, my response was "I know." Why would I be like Laura? Why would Bill choose to date a woman who was exactly like the wife he had lost?

I also thought a lot about how uncomfortable I was back then. When one half of a good marriage dies, there are no hard feelings like there can be after a divorce or a bad break up. No one is going to speak badly of the person who passed, and understandably so. Because of this, I felt like Laura was a saint and that there was no way I could ever live up to that. I was human and I had flaws. She was gone and would forever be the ideal. It was an impossible standard to hold myself to.

Of course, Bill never once compared us. I was doing it to myself out of my own insecurities.

One day Bill mentioned a situation in which Laura had not been very patient and I burst out laughing and said, "So she was human?" Hearing this one flaw about her made me feel like she was not the saint I'd conjured up, but a real, live person.

I kept this in mind as Eric and I began to see each other. I spoke freely of Bill all the time, but I made sure not to unwittingly canonize him. While I had no control over how Eric chose to internalize what I said, I wanted to be clear that Bill was a human, with a wide range of human characteristics and that I loved him deeply because of it.

I'd be painting a false picture if I didn't say that October also brought many dark nights. I was alone in my place in Cambria, with no job and no idea of what my future held. I felt lost more often than not. I knew my schedule wasn't sustainable. I'd have to go back to work eventually and that would limit my time. What did I want my life to look like? I couldn't figure it out yet. I wasn't there. I wanted my family back, and that was the one thing I couldn't have.

⚶

Our weekend in San Francisco arrived. It felt good to be back in the city and I was beyond excited to go to the opera. I'm not a fanatic, but I do appreciate the pomp and circumstance of it all. It also afforded me an excuse to get dressed up, and I loved getting complimented on the vintage outfit I pieced together.

It was the first time I'd seen Eric in dress clothes. I was floored. He was gorgeous! I had helped him find the tie and jacket but hadn't see it all together. I preened, knowing we looked good together.

We had a fantastic dinner before we made our way to the opera house. We both marveled that the day was so slow and unhurried. Once there, we explored the gorgeous old building before finding our seats. It was The Marriage of Figaro and we both loved it.

The weekend rolled on from there. We explored museums and went on a self-guided nosh crawl of North Beach before popping down to Oakland for Dom's 50th birthday. It was time together without being fraught with moving and sadness and stress. It was perfect.

On the drive back to the Central Coast, I wondered why I was leaving him for a month.

But I knew I had to.

16

landed in Paris on a cold grey morning after a bizarre overnight flight. I
was seated in the middle of the plane, surrounded by acrobats. Normally
would love that but they were all about 25 years younger than I and very
talkative. I chatted with a few of the women near me but after a while
exhaustion overcame me. They kept the party rolling and I was envious of
their enthusiasm for life.

It felt so good to be back in Paris. I'd been there maybe a dozen times
at that point, most recently in 2014 when Bill and I had taken a trip from
Paris to Berlin. It's an easy place to be for me because it's comfortable
and familiar while still being a world away from home. I had majored in
French and I speak well enough to survive beyond "Where is the toilet?"

I met up with Manu at a café to get the keys to his parents' apartment.
Once there, I collapsed from fatigue. Flights from California are a whole
lot longer than they are from New York. I slept for a bit, then forced
myself out into the city. I walked over towards Notre Dame to see what it
looked like after the fire, then popped into Shakespeare & Co. to load up
on books. Nearby is Église St Julien le Pauvre, a small 13th century church
where concerts are often held. I saw that a piano concert was coming up
that included some Gershwin. I bought a ticket immediately.

I wandered all over the city and finally returned home, tired, happy, and ready for the deep sleep that had eluded me since March 7th.

※

I hadn't slept much during my lost month of September. Instead I had often stayed up late researching places to go after Paris. I wanted to take advantage of the cheap flights in Europe and extend my trip to include a few more stops. Maybe I felt that if I could go far away, I'd get out of my head and away from my own pain.

This trip also afforded me the luxury of time. I'd never had so much time to be able to spend in Paris. I was staying at the Manu's parents' apartment, so I didn't have to worry about expensive accommodations adding up.

I considered Spain, but it felt too awful to think about going back when Bill and I had just gone the year before. Italy was possible, but we'd been saving that as a trip together so that was out too. Croatia was a little far, and I didn't want to go anywhere north since we were heading into winter. I finally settled on Lisbon. Then I thought to myself "If I'm going to Lisbon, I'll be close to Morocco too... why not head there?" I freely admit to falling for the romanticized version of Marrakech portrayed in pop culture, particularly during the 1970s. Done. Booked.

I wasn't paying attention to dates, I guess, because I booked my flight or Lisbon for the day after I arrived in Paris.

In the early morning hours, a car came to pick me up and bring me to he airport. Once I was at my gate, I sat back to enjoy people-watching. realized that one of the reasons I booked so many flights was that I eeded to be comfortable in airports again.

It had never occurred to me how much the Miami airport had scarred ne. Since I was normally very private, the middle of a crowded airport vas probably the worst possible place to learn that my husband had ust died. I used to love airports – the anticipation of travel, the people-vatching, the dozens of languages. I loved having a beer and chatting with ther travelers.

While it was certainly too early for a beer, I felt some of my old xcitement return as I sat there and watched the bustling terminal. To be ble to feel that excitement again told me that I might just live through his after all.

I landed in Lisbon about three hours before I could check into my irbnb. My ass was kicked from jetlag. My cab driver from the airport lidn't speak English, so I tried French and then Spanish. He begrudgingly responded. I didn't want to push it; Spain and Portugal have a long, complicated, and often bloody history. Still, it was encouraging that Spanish was available in a pinch.

I lugged my backpack up a narrow alley to find the Airbnb. A small square a few blocks away seemed like a good place to hangout for a while, and I watched as craft vendors began to set up. Café workers pulled out tables and opened awnings. It was fun to watch a city I didn't know get ready for the day.

I spent four days in Lisbon.

My first night I attended a fado concert that included wine and tapas. It was one of the best nights I'd had in a while. The host, Humberto, was a fado aficionado and his enthusiasm was contagious. When I told him that I worked in wine, he put me in touch with a sommelier friend of his.

The concert itself was incredible. The singer's voice was so haunting and emotional that I fell in love with fado myself. Most of the attendees were also women, some traveling alone, and it felt so good for my soul to be surrounded by other curious beings from around the world. I went back to my apartment that night with a heart full of happiness and gratitude, something I had not felt in a long time.

The next day, I went on a walking tour of Alfama. I had the afternoon free to explore even more and found a huge flea market, which was heaven to me. I'm fortunate to not get lonely easily, so I delighted in eating out by myself and watching the world go by.

For my last full day in Portugal, I booked a tour of Sintra. My driver was from Serbia, so our conversations were very literal and limited. We visited Quinta da Regaleira and Montserrate Palace before heading to Boca Inferno, or 'the mouth of hell,' a grotto that makes demonic sounds under the right wind conditions. That day didn't allow for it, but it was a beautiful location. From there, we went to the westernmost point on the European continent. It was a moody, grey day and the wind had the ocean whipped up. I loved every second of it and imagined the sheer badassedness of European explorers setting off into the vast unknown.

The day ended in Cascaís, a tiny town on the coast. The driver dropped me off and told me to meet him back in an hour. I explored and ended up in a clothing store. Knowing that everything I'd brought still had to make it through a few days in Marrakech, I bought a dress right off the rack. At least I'd have something unsmelly to wear if necessary.

The next morning I packed up and headed back to the airport, feeling little sad that I'd had such a short time in Lisbon.

Landing in Marrakech was a dream come true. I'd always wanted to go to Morocco but never thought it would actually happen. Bill and I had considered it when we were planning Barcelona, but it seemed like a lot to add to an already busy trip. Besides, Bill had little interest in going anywhere in Africa. This would be my first time.

Something about landing in a completely different environment thrilled me. It was both disconcerting and freeing to be around a language that didn't resemble any I knew. I had to turn my brain off from trying to decipher signs – there was no way I'd magically decode Arabic on my own.

Thanks to colonization, though, everything in the Marrakech airport was also in French and English. I followed fellow passengers through immigration and customs and spilled out into the open terminal. The exterior walls were an elaborate metal design that resembled ornate Arabic engraving and calligraphy. It was entrancing.

I followed the crowd to currency exchange and got some money, then left the terminal and attempted to find the driver sent by the riad, the traditional hotel where I'd be staying. A tall man held up a sign with my name and greeted me with a warm "Welcome to Ahfreekah!"

I was smitten.

As he drove to the medina, traffic grew thicker. We turned in towards the old city and cars gave way to throngs of people. While I had known in theory that the medina would be crowded, to see it in real time was another experience entirely. We drove slowly, though the driver didn't seem overly concerned about hitting anyone. We passed through an open-air market with every kind of fruit, vegetable, and meat out for sale, along with dusty piles of books, sandals, and everything else anyone could need. At one of the doors leading into the walled portion of the city, we pulled over and the driver told me to follow him.

We went through the gate and arrived at a huge, forbidding door. He slammed the knocker loudly. To my very American eyes, this was an unusual way for a hotel to have visitors announce their presence but hell. We weren't in America.

Inside we were greeted by Whalid, the concierge, who invited me to sit and presented small cookies and mint tea that he poured with a flourish. He ambled back behind the desk to pull out paperwork and it struck me how relaxed and unhurried the process was. I felt like I could just breathe and be.

My room faced the street, but all of the pedestrian noise evaporated as soon as I closed the heavy shutters. As I settled in, I heard the call to prayer. My whole body reverberated. I'd heard it before in Brooklyn, where there had been a mosque near my apartment, but never this loudly.

I lay down on the bed and mulled over what to do. I was intimidated at the thought of going out by myself, concerned about being a woman traveling alone in north Africa. I also didn't have a map that made sense. When all of the streets are narrow and winding, trying to match up names across Arabic and English gets complicated quickly. I decided to stay at the riad that evening and regroup.

At dinner that night I had a local wine that was fine and a wonderful conversation with the night concierge, Abdullah. He was in college and loved literature. When he heard my accent, he jumped at the chance to talk. I attempted to speak French with him but he switched back to English and politely said "Madam, we younger people do not like to speak French because it was from a hard time." I apologized and stuck to English. We ended up chatting for about two hours. My solo dinner turned out to be anything but and I returned to my room happy and grateful for his gesture of friendship.

The next morning I braced myself for the Arabian market, called a souk. I was still trying to regain my confidence, but didn't want to waste my trip spending time at the riad.

Whalid was back on shift that day and walked me over to a huge map on the wall. He traced exactly where I should go. I asked how to get to the route he had pointed out and he said "Turn right, then left." I doubted these detailed instructions until I got out into the street and saw that yes, I really did just turn right and then left.

I made said right and left and the street opened up to a broader avenue. Ok, 'avenue' is being generous, but it was wider than most other streets around the riad. I paid close attention to different buildings and signs that I passed, relying on landmarks rather than signs or directions. I have no sense of north or south but I can find restaurants I visited ten years before if the surrounding landmarks have stayed the same.

I plunged further into the city and eventually found myself in the souk. Every kind of vendor imaginable was there, selling leather slippers, rings, ceramic tiles, fresh meat, water, long garments, lanterns, incense, oils, spices, rugs, ice, sweets, chips – everything. "Signora!" they would call to me, followed by "Madam!" and "Senora!" I kept my sunglasses on to avoid eye contact, but loved that I wasn't standing out as American. I wanted to blend in as much as possible.

⋇

The day grew busier and hotter. The sun was now fully up and the streets were clogged with pedestrians, motorcyclists, cars, donkeys, and trucks. Never before had I seen a near miss between a donkey and a truck.

The street I was on had some construction and one of the men working ordered me to turn around and not continue. Without a working map, I didn't know where to go other than back towards my riad.

A police officer approached me. In perfect English, he asked "Madam, where are you trying to go?" I explained that I was just exploring, not looking for anything in particular. "Would you like to see some carpets? That building is where they are made." He pointed to a nondescript edifice a couple of paces away. Sure, why not.

He led me in and spoke rapid Arabic to a tall, well-dressed man inside.

"Please, come this way!" I walked into a large room. There were balconies on the walls around us. Hanging over the balustrades were carpets of every possible color and design. It was an incredible riot of color.

"Would you like to see how they're made?" he asked me. Damn right I would! He led me through another hallway to a room where a woman about my age was weaving on an enormous loom. She worked quickly, tying small pieces of wool thread in rapid succession on a long vertical strand. The manager stopped her so she could show me how she did it. "Would you like to try?" I laughed and politely declined; I was not about to mess up her gorgeous handiwork with my ineptitude.

The manager showed me some rugs for purchase. I admired a few but didn't want to waste his time – I certainly wasn't buying anything. I thanked him for his time and headed back into the souk, delighted at the outcome of my construction-induced turnaround.

As I began to make my way back towards the riad, I thought about the officer and the carpet manager. I travel a lot by myself, so of course I've had unfortunate experiences. There was a nasty situation in Bucharest when a man followed me for a while before I could lose him. Another time, in Tobago, a local insisted I should follow him into a forest to buy some fruit (I did not). I'm certainly not naïve when I travel, and I try to get a feel for my surroundings and the people I'm interacting with. I had no way of knowing if the police officer was actually an officer, but we were out in the open and there were other women around, so it felt worth trusting him enough to hear him out. Similarly, the carpet shop manager was gracious and kept a reasonable distance so I did not feel uncomfortable in the building. Sometimes, it's worth taking the leap of trust.

The evening landed me on a rooftop terrace from which I could see the mosque tower directly. I ordered a glass of wine and listened to the evening call to prayer, relishing every moment.

The next morning, I woke up with a raging sore throat. I couldn't believe how sick I'd gotten in only 12 hours. I tried to fix myself up as much as I could, but I was in rough shape.

As I made my way back towards the souk I was side-tracked by a spice shop. Even while congested, the incredible scent drew me in. The young man working stopped me and said "Madam! May I?" as he held up a roller ball of orange blossom oil. I nodded yes and he rubbed it around my temples and my hair line. "This is good to relax," he explained. He then held out a small gauze square and sprinkled in some nigella seeds and some other little crystals, twisted it, and tied it. He positioned it under my right nostril and sealed off the other with his hand. "Breathe" he said, and WOW! It felt like a snooter of Tiger's Balm and my head immediately cleared out. I bought some orange blossom oil and he gave me the gauze packet to take home.

It occurred to me as soon as I left that, much like in my 20s, I had just snorted something a stranger told me to – only this time I wasn't in a dingy bathroom on the Lower East Side. Maturity has its perks.

Later that day, I ventured back out in search of Jardin Majorelle, a garden beyond the walls of the old city. I passed through the chaos of the market and arrived at a major boulevard. I couldn't find a cross walk, but the locals seemed to wait for a small pack to form, cross once there was a break in traffic, and hope for the best. It worked.

There was a long queue for the Jardin, so I went to the Yves Saint Laurent Museum first. I certainly don't consider myself a fashionista, but I love fashion's place in art history and there's no questioning Saint-Laurent's influence. A Mondrian-inspired dress from his 1965 collection hovered above the entrance and I damn near lost my mind. I dove into the haute couture archives for a while, enjoying the cool, dark interior of the museum almost as much as the works of art.

Jardin Majorelle was hypnotically beautiful. Searing cobalt blue blanketed all the structures and lush greenery enveloped every footpath. It was complete peace and serenity and a fitting place for Saint-Laurent's ashes to reside.

My final day in Marrakech found me feeling ballsy enough to push even further into the "new" city. I made my morning rounds in the souk and then ventured back beyond the wall. I stopped for lunch at Grand

Café de la Presse, a throwback to French colonialism, where I had a killer niçoise for lunch.

While I wasn't thrilled about another series of flights, I was happy to land back in Paris the following evening and fall into bed, where I could sleep as late as I needed to the next morning.

Paris was cold and rainy, but it didn't matter to me. I relished my morning stop at a café and grabbed a croissant from the corner boulangerie. I did nothing that first day but wash some clothes and read. It was perfect.

The next day was the church concert. Manu took half a day and we went out exploring the city together. The temperature dropped and the rain turned to icy sleet. I was drenched. We stopped in a brasserie for a small bite before he headed to a dinner party and I went to the concert. I fortified myself with some red wine at a bar next door as I waited for it to start, fearing the church would not be heated.

After the doors opened I nestled into a seat in the first row. One bonus to traveling alone is that it's easy to get great seats when you only need one. The pianist came out and began her performance. After a few pieces, she stood up and told us that she was from Japan and had adapted ancient cherry blossom music for the piano. She began to play again and I froze. It was the exact music my brother had given me twenty years before on a CD he'd gotten while living in Japan. I loved the music so much that it was one of the only CDs I still owned, despite having moved so frequently. I listened with every cell in my body.

What happened next astonished me: her very next piece was Gershwin's "Rhapsody in Blue," which is what Bill and I were married to. To have my world colliding across decades and continents made every hair on my body stand up and I almost wept with gratitude.

After my return to Paris, the loneliness crept up on me again. Manu worked during the day and outside of work he had a life. I didn't want to demand much of his time. A friend from San Francisco was going to be in town soon, but I wasn't sure if we'd be able to connect. At first, I took advantage of my freedom to explore Paris in a way I never had before. Previous solo trips were usually for about a week, and I'd always packed in a lot. This was the first visit in which I was both alone and had as much time as I wanted.

But, I realized, I did miss structure. Every day I'd map out what I wanted to see, but I'd let myself get distracted if something more interesting popped up. I visited countless museums that I hadn't before and even discovered a few new favorites. I steeped myself in holiday consumerism by diving into Galeries Lafayette and Bon Marché. I popped into cafes and bistros by myself to warm up over a class of wine or a café au lait. But I tired easily, and often I found myself on the other side of the city, completely exhausted and not looking forward to the long trek back to the apartment by myself.

Despite the exhaustion, I walked a lot while I was there, averaging about 12 miles per day. Physically working my body helped me work through tough emotions.

Manu invited me out often. I didn't always go. Since Bill's death I'd been pushing so hard to build my life back up that I needed time to rest.

However, I did go out for Manu's girlfriend's birthday at a bar on the other side of the city. When I arrived, the party had taken over multiple tables and about 20 people were there chatting happily with each other. There was also group of acapella singers, all dressed up in sparkles and glitter, singing pop hits from the 70s and 80s. I looked at Manu with my eyebrows raised and he just said "I have no idea what is going on!" It was hilarious.

Since I didn't want to monopolize Manu's time, I attempted to make small talk with the people sitting on either side of me. The man to my left was probably in his late 50s and his English was about as proficient as my French; while we both could understand a basic conversation, we lacked the vocabulary for more nuanced discussion.

He asked how long I was staying in Paris and I said a month, at least. He asked what I did for work that allowed me to be there for so long. I explained my job a little, but added that I wasn't working because it had been a very difficult year. Apparently the French understand the need for mental health leave, because he agreed a month was a good break. Then he asked the question that I'd been dreading since I landed: Was I alone? Where was my husband?

I'd actually thought this through before the trip, but in the heat of conversation I lost the more elegant phrases I'd concocted and blurted out "Mort. Mon mari est mort."

Needless to say, my conversation partner was not anticipating that. He looked shocked and then a little embarrassed. "But you are young for this, no?" he said. I nodded in agreement. He asked me how my husband died and I said "Je ne sais pas la phrase en français mais... une crise du coeur?"

The bluntness of my revelation later stuck in my mind. In English, I likely would have said something like "Well I was married for almost five years but my husband passed away suddenly this past March..." It would have been wordier, but it would have been a much softer blow for my conversation partner. But there was something very freeing about lacking the words that would have allowed me to equivocate my position. I was forced to be harsh and direct. To say that my husband "passed away" sounds as though he just slipped out. He didn't. He died - suddenly, shockingly, harshly. Il est mort.

Manu and I had planned to spend the week of Thanksgiving in Nice and Corsica. We were going to visit his parents near Nice, borrow their car, and ferry over to Corsica from there. About a week and a half before we were due to leave Paris, I woke up in a panic about the trip. Something was telling me not to go. I was having trouble breathing at the thought of it. I had the same feeling I'd had before Klaus was killed. I decided to sleep on it but the next day the feeling was worse. I told Manu I had to cancel.

He wasn't happy, but he said "I can't imagine what you've been through this year, so if you are not comfortable going we can cancel."

thanked him and changed my ticket home to an earlier date.

The night we were supposed to have arrived in Corsica, Manu and I ate out in Paris. He said "Oh, I forgot to tell you! Our ferry was canceled. It seems that extreme weather shut all of Corsica down and the mayor declared a state of emergency. We wouldn't have been able to get there."

I stared at him. WHAT was going on?! Why was I getting these feelings? As I was trying to process, Manu's mother called him from Nice because his father had fallen ill and was in the hospital. Manu excused himself and made a series of calls to family members, agreeing to head south first thing in the morning.

I was shaken up that my intuition had been so accurate.

17

The four months off from work brought a lot of soul searching, more than I ever thought I was capable of. I was never spiritual before, but I definitely learned to tune in. Why not? Nothing I had known made sense anymore, so everything else was now a possibility.

Immediately after Bill died, I sought grief counseling and support because I was such a mess. I was surprised by how few services there were for younger widows. A friend referred me to an online group that was helpful at first, but every time a newbie joined I felt like I was reliving the trauma all over again. Yoga and hiking were helpful, and as I realized just how much I began to rethink my career. I briefly considered returning to school to become a grief counselor, but having to earn another Master's was too overwhelming to consider. Then, while on the phone with Dom one night, he asked "Hey, have you ever considered becoming a life coach? I think you'd be fantastic."

A life coach? I thought. *Were they even legit?* Dom told me that he was one and that he found it to be a valuable and rewarding experience. It was an interesting thought. A few days later, my aunt asked me the same thing. I hadn't told her my career concerns at all.

Around the same time, my real estate agent asked if she could put me in touch with a friend who was a life coach. At this point I was genuinely curious.

The coach, Nalani, was crucial to figuring out my next steps because I had no idea what to do. When confronted with unlimited choices, people often don't end up choosing at all. We don't know where to begin.

Nalani called me and we talked through where I was. I broke down several times. She asked me how I wanted my life to look and I said "I just want to be able to talk about Bill and Klaus without losing it." That was it, but that was everything.

Nalani was a gift. During one of our sessions, she asked me what I would have if I could have anything at all. I knew the answer: A wellness studio. As my experience with yoga had evolved, I had realized there were countless ways to interpret mindfulness and meditative practices, all of which could help others suffering through loss and grief. Nalani told me to brainstorm all of the things I wanted to do and then look back over it for any themes or repetitions. Yoga came up several times - becoming a yoga teacher, having a studio, and running retreats around the world.

Back in June, I'd booked a retreat in Zanzibar for early 2020. I knew that if I made it through the holidays in one piece, I was going to need a major mental and physical break.

Then my friend Claudia sent me the info on a yoga retreat run by one of her friends. Her trip to visit me in Lake County hadn't happened because I left so quickly after moving there, so she wondered if I wanted to meet her in Sicily in June. Was it crazy to return to work in January, only to leave twice in the next six months? Probably, but I didn't care. I booked that as well. Then I asked the host if she'd be interested in having wine pairings or classes during the week. I wanted to see if there was a way to combine my love and expertise in wine with my passion for yoga. She loved the idea and we began to hash out details.

My yoga practice continued to grow, as did my strength and flexibility. For the first time in my life, I'd lose track of time during a practice. My thoughts were unfocused, allowing my mind to wander free when I was on the mat.

I began to think seriously about becoming a teacher. I had always told myself not to spend loads of money on something that was just a hobby when I already had a safe job. But after a while, safe didn't cut it anymore. The urge to try something different kept pulling at my fingertips. Signs continued to pop up, and I'd been learning to listen a whole lot more.

After I moved to Cambria, my friend Laura connected me with her friend Julie. We met up for a drink one evening at a bistro in the village. She was about my age, very mellow and laid-back, and we chatted about where we were in life. She was in the process of moving down to Mexico and I expressed my admiration. She invited me down to her place once it was finished. She talked of wanting to quit her job and I said I was in the same boat.

"When do you have to decide?" she asked. I said not until January because I was off until then.

"Why don't you just become a yoga teacher? You seem like you'd be good!" she said. This stunned me – we hadn't even discussed yoga. She'd gleaned my interest from social media but even there, I only post about yoga occasionally. I smiled and said I'd consider it.

18

The holidays were coming up, which meant that the anniversary of my wedding to Bill — December 28th — was approaching. I was still trying to figure out how to handle it. Eric offered for me to join him near his parents, but it felt like too much too soon. Instead, we drove down to Los Angeles together and I headed further south from there. My first stop was in Long Beach with my friends Mickey and Tommy. Mickey and I had met because of our dogs. Shortly after we adopted Klaus, I was walking him one morning along 4th Avenue and saw a woman walking towards me with a Jack Russell who looked like a negative image of Klaus - white where Klaus was black. The two dogs dragged us towards each other and began to play right there like they were long lost brothers. It was adorable and hilarious, and Mickey and I had playdates for the dogs from then on. She and her husband Tommy became like family to us and invited us over often.

Mickey adored Klaus almost as much as we did. When I'd called her to tell her that he'd died she cried bitterly over the phone. It was hard to go to their place, but I wanted to be around her. Their dog Dante raced towards me when I arrived and it felt so good to be with Klaus's best friend. He curled up in my lap every chance he could and I loved feeling that warm little body against mine.

⸻

December 28th was difficult. Bill and I had gotten married between Christmas and New Year's because his wife Laura died on New Year's Eve and my father died on Christmas day. We thought "Hey, let's change the tone of the holidays!" but without him and without Klaus, it was unbearable.

A few days before, I arrived in San Diego to stay at my aunt's. When got there, I visited Balboa Park to check out a few museums. The park was packed with tourists who were off for Christmas break. Food trucks lined the avenue and musicians and craft vendors were set up. One table was asking for donations in exchange for books about yoga and meditation. looked over a few. Even though I'd practiced yoga for years, I didn't know anything about the philosophy or theory behind it.

One of the young men working the table asked me "Are you a yoga instructor?" I was stunned. Why would he even ask that? I was just bumming around in jeans and a t-shirt — nothing particularly screamed "YOGA INSTRUCTOR" about me. I smiled and said "No — why?" He looked me over and replied "You just look like you'd make a great yogi."

The universe had my attention.

On the 28th itself, I went to Anza Borrego. It's an otherworldly California State Park with dozens of huge metal sculptures dotting the desert landscape. My favorite was a dragon whose body is interwoven with the land. Having a snarling face-off with him seemed appropriate for such a hard day. I left feeling oddly empowered. It felt like I had mentally shifted to face the rest of my life.

honey

/ˈhənē/

Definition of *honey*

1a: *a sweet viscid material elaborated out of the nectar of flowers in the honey sac of various bees*

b: *a sweet fluid resembling honey that is collected or elaborated by various insects*

2a: *a loved one : SWEETHEART, DEAR*

b: *a superlative example*

3: *the quality or state of being sweet : SWEETNESS*

you (can) catch more flies with honey than (with) vinegar

sweet as honey

the land of milk and honey

19

January first arrived. In years past I had looked forward to the mental reset but this time I knew that didn't exist. I was facing a new year in which neither Bill nor Klaus would exist anywhere other than my mind.

Bill was my biggest teacher in those moments. When I met him, he'd lost Laura two years earlier and had dealt with a lot of employment upheaval. It would have been completely understandable if he was bitter about it, but he simply wasn't. It wasn't in his nature. He treated life as an adventure; it was something we connected over. We tried to always be open to whatever happened and hilarity often ensued. Losing that part of us didn't seem like an option, and understanding his love of life on a visceral level deepened my own.

Bill understood something that I'd only realized during our marriage: no one can make someone else happy. No one. We can only make ourselves happy. Bill was the best example I'd ever seen of someone at peace with who he was.

I had to let that sink in. By then Eric and I were in a relationship, and wanted to be clear-headed about my reasons for being with him. Was I expecting him to save me from something? Was I expecting him to "make" me happy?

Back from Europe and past the holidays, I settled into my new place and started to build my schedule. I went to the gym almost every morning. I was back to work, and Eric and I only saw each other on the weekends. That was fine with me because my place was small and he and his dog Ichi were two added bodies in a tight space. I loved seeing him, but I also loved having a space that was totally MINE, something I hadn't experienced in over ten years. It would get hauntingly quiet at times. I had to sort through the silence on my own and not expect anyone to fill it up. That shit right there was powerful.

The new year presented the opportunity of Dry January. I was determined to participate, which was a big deal for me. I come from a long line of alcoholics. My paternal grandfather was a heavy drinker who died in his 40s of a massive heart attack; my father claimed it was from smoking but the alcoholism surely didn't help. My father followed suit and drank himself in and out of hospitals for the last 15 years of his life before dying of organ failure at 64. Alcoholism feels like it is, in a sense, my birthright.

In light of this, perhaps it seems curious that I chose wine as my profession. But for me it made perfect sense: I wanted to understand how drink. After a lifetime of seeing vodka compulsively gulped like water at 10am, I wanted to figure out how other people could stop drinking whenever they chose. I made my way through several wine certification programs and gained a certain amount of expertise. I knew what wine to pair with any dish. Bill was a chef and every night we'd delight in picking out wine from our cellar to pair with whatever he'd made that evening.

That, though: "Every night." That was the problem.

What I'd thought would help me understand how to control it instead led me to drink way too much. Working in wine normalized daily drinking. We usually polished off a bottle with dinner, and soon started to indulge in a nightcap too.

I never missed a day of work, I never drank on the job – rare, in the industry – and I certainly never drank the way my father did.

But the thought of not drinking scared me. Looking back, I was a functioning alcoholic. I justified it by saying I'd had a long day, or I needed to unwind, or some other bullshit excuse. Bill never called me out; he didn't need to, because the alcohol was taking its toll. I gained weight and my energy dropped, especially because I was often operating with a low-grade hangover.

And after Bill died? I drank.

I didn't drink that night in the Miami hotel as I waited out the terrible hours before my flight home. I didn't even drink on the flight. But the moment I walked through my door Junior poured me glass after glass in the hopes that I'd be able to finally get some sleep.

This became a habit. The combination of my grief and my profession had friends excusing how much I drank. "Oh, you're not that bad," one assured me. "I've seen people drink way more than you, and you're going through so much!"

It was true. But the only people drinking more than I did were serious alcoholics.

When I finally began to emerge from the paralyzing grief that followed his death, I consciously decided that I had to face my fears if I was going to heal. I dealt with banks, home improvement, moving, and real estate agents myself. I took time off work and traveled alone to countries where I didn't know anyone and didn't speak the language.

And then I decided to tackle alcohol.

I set December 31st as the last day I would drink for at least a month. Eric agreed to give it a go along with me. Over the holidays I indulged in Manhattans, beer, and entirely too much wine, which culminated in crushing hangover on New Year's Day.

In the beginning, I missed the habit of having a glass of wine as I cooked dinner. I soon realized that I didn't miss much beyond that. By the end of the first week I'd lost 3 pounds. I had more energy and felt better than I had in years.

I thought about what I'd been scared of. I'd been scared of not being able to sleep; I'd worried that the grief from the year would come crashing back down on me. Most of all, I was terrified of the physical withdrawal.

By week two, things began to shift. My energy levels evened out, I was sleeping better than I had in years, and my workouts felt great - but I was often tired and cranky by the end of the day. In week three, something happened that made me pay attention. I had a shitty day, and by the evening was so frustrated that I thought "Fuck it! I'm going to have some wine!"

But I didn't drink, because my impulse to turn to alcohol after a bad day was frightening.

Drinking to go numb was the danger zone. Wine had once been about flavor and pairings and dinners for me, but at some point it became my drug of choice. I had started in the wine industry because I loved it, but the easy access allowed it to seep into every aspect of my life, including how I coped with grief or anger.

January also meant going back to work, which I'd been dreading.
knew I had to return – I needed the income and health insurance. It als
felt like my life had been in a holding pattern for almost a year. Every tim
I made progress something would push me back into a terrible limbo. Wit
everything feeling so unstable, work was the only certainty in my life.

It was good to be back with my team again and getting some muc
needed human interaction, even if it was only virtual. But I'd find myse
drifting off a lot throughout the day, sometimes taking a yoga class while
was working. I knew I didn't care about the job anymore and that it woul
show eventually. I prided myself on having a reputation as a hard work
and returning felt like I was risking that.

We were also in a holding pattern with the sale of the house. It ha
been on the market since September, but it was expensive for the area an
it had an odd layout. It had been perfect for Bill and me, but it require
the right person and we still hadn't found anyone. By January I was losin
patience. I was paying rent on my apartment and the utilities and taxes o
a house in which I didn't live.

In January we finally got an offer, but the buyers weren't ready to pu
the trigger because they had to sell their place on the other side of th

country. I was worried. The longer it was drawn out, the more it felt like the deal was going to fall through altogether.

I told myself I was okay and I was getting through it. I was "fine." I woke up early every morning to go to the gym, then would work or take a yoga class or write. But I still felt trapped by inertia. My job was dull and repetitive, the sale of my house was at a standstill, and I was still struggling to figure out what I was going to do with my life.

My neck grew incredibly stiff and painful. It hurt to stretch, and finally went to an acupuncturist for the first time. She listened silently, nodding along, while I explained everything that had happened. I was nervous when she led me over to the table. I had no idea what to expect, but it didn't hurt. Afterwards, I thought "Hm, ok, well that was weird," but didn't notice much of a change.

At least not until that night, when I wept like Bill had just died in front of me. I couldn't sleep. My body heaved with wave after wave of grief. I finally fell asleep around 4 am.

I emailed Jennifer as soon as I woke up. "Was that supposed to happen? What the hell?!" She replied immediately. "Yes. You weren't letting yourself experience your grief because you were 'fine.' Your body was storing it. How do you feel this morning?"

I realized that my neck was loose and I felt lighter, more buoyant. I was stunned. She was absolutely right; she'd targeted my grief and allowed me to purge it.

I began to focus on the trip to Zanzibar, which was coming up at the end of February. I applied for the visas and got the recommended vaccines. My upper left arm swelled up from the shots. It hurt like hell, but it was fun that that one section of my body looked like I'd been working out on steroids. Plus, there was something badass about knowing I was medically bulletproof.

January was a tough month. I had too much time to think. I knew that my old normal was gone forever and I would have to build a new one, but often found myself wanting to leap forward a year to be IN it already.

But that's not the way life works.

I began to realize that I couldn't keep running to escape myself. It had been about 6 months since I'd lost Klaus and almost a year since I lost Bill. Reality was hitting me. This was life now.

I also struggled to interact with people around me. I heard, over and over, things like "It's time to move on" or "I'm glad you're moving on."

But there was no moving on. I would never be a person who hadn't loved and lost Bill. Moving on was a ludicrous concept to me, like I was expected to pack up part of my heart and put it in my storage unit.

I felt like I was fundamentally different. I didn't think the same way, or interact with people the same way. My bandwidth for manufactured drama was nonexistent. I noticed that there were people in my life who tended to focus on the negative and I began to disengage from them, leaving texts, voicemails, and messages unanswered. And I got it, I truly did: we all had a lot going on, all the time. But I was in no shape to soothe someone else's ego.

19

In February, I came to an emotional turning point. I knew that traveling wasn't financially sustainable and wallowing wasn't emotionally sustainable. I couldn't stay at my job and continue with everything like it was the same as ever, because I was not the same and there was no returning to the woman I had been in March 2019. And I was tired. I was tired down to my bones.

Around this time, Eric asked me if I would consider moving in together. My first thought was "why not?", and my second thought was "But what will people think?!" I knew all too well that people had opinions about what my life should look like. I told him that I was tired of moving, but if we happened to see something that was a perfect fit I'd consider it.

February also saw the end of my coaching sessions with Nalani. We'd talked through my wants and had a rough plan to follow for the rest of the year. I would start coaching certification when I got back from Zanzibar, which I would pay for with money from the sale of my house.

As the Zanzibar trip drew closer, my spirits brightened. I was scared but excited, ready to break my holding pattern with the invigorating experience of traveling somewhere new. At the same time, I didn't want to leave Eric so soon. We'd just started seeing each other when I left in

November, and by the time I got back the holidays hit. Here I was, gearing up to leave again just a month and a half later. I asked him point blank if he would get tired of me always coming and going. He told me "This is who you are. If you decide to leave for a year, ok, we might have a problem, but I would never expect you to change who you are for me."

In the weeks before my departure, news began to break about Coronavirus. China was going into lockdown. At first I paid it no mind. But by mid-February it started to sound serious and I began to wonder if I should cancel the trip.

In the meantime, Eric sent me the link to a house for rent in Cambria. "I know you aren't ready," he wrote "But is it worth looking at this?" It was a beautiful Tudor-style cottage five minutes away from my apartment, complete with a fireplace and a yard. The owners allowed pets.

We made an appointment to see it and I explained to the landlord that we weren't in any hurry. As soon as we got there, we realized it was perfect. Eric decided he was going to take it no matter what and that I could move in when my lease was up.

Two days before my departure for Zanzibar, I got sick. It felt exactly like what had happened in Marrakech: it came out of nowhere and within

2 hours I was congested. I loaded up on every remedy I could think of and tried to sleep it off.

20

When I landed in Dar es Salaam, I realized I'd missed my flight to Zanzibar because I'd miscalculated time zones. The terminal with the office for puddle jumpers was closed, so I asked some guys standing outside if they knew what to do. One told me to give him the cash and he'd get the ticket. I thought What sort of chump do you think I am? But the reality was that I could either trust him or be stuck in Dar overnight. I'd already been traveling for 30 hours and was exhausted. The sun felt unnaturally bright. I handed over the cash and he disappeared into the terminal.

I waited and waited. My back was aching. I saw him at the other end of the terminal, chatting away with some friends. The fuck... I walked over to him. He said there was a flight leaving soon and he was trying to get me on it. After a few more minutes of negotiation, he disappeared into the building again and came out with a ticket for me. I was stunned.

I thanked him several times and hopped on the shuttle to the terminal. There was another passenger who had missed his flight riding with us and it turned out that we would be seated next to each other.

The puddle jumper terminal was bare bones. As we waited to board the propeller plane, I chatted a bit with the other passenger. He offered to show me around Stone Town in Zanzibar if I had the time and gave me his phone number.

When I finally landed, I'd missed my ride to the retreat by a few hours. I had no way to contact the resort. I walked out to the group of taxi drivers and asked them if anyone knew Paje by Night. One offered to call them for me and ask about getting me a ride. Similar to Dar, I waited around and watched what felt like complete inaction. I realized how American was, assuming that nothing was happening unless everyone was showing urgency. Soon enough my driver showed up and flagged me down.

Paje was on the other side of the island, which I hadn't realized, so it took about an hour to get there. But finally, finally, I arrived and found myself in paradise.

Yoga class was the next morning at 8 am, in a studio about three steps away from my bungalow. It was already hot and the humidity was intense. I came to accept that I would be sweating all the time. I grabbed a mat and settled in near a window.

Our instructor, Dikla, was younger than I. She was lean and muscular and held herself with fierce strength. I was immediately intimidated. As she spoke to the class it became clear that some students had been there for a while and others, like myself, had just arrived.

I supposed I thought it would all be soft and soothing. But when

Dikla began our practice, I realized that was not the case. She insisted on perfect form from the start. She corrected everything from the exact placement of our hands to the length of our inhales. I didn't know if I wanted to put myself through this for 90 minutes twice per day. As we wrapped up, Dikla showed us all how to set up for a headstand and then walked around helping individuals invert. I'd only ever done shoulder stands before and even then, it had been many years since I had last attempted one. She walked us through the set up but that was as far as I went that morning. No way was I going to get up into a headstand!

I spent the rest of the day exploring the area around our resort and recovering from jetlag. I was dreading another class but when the time came Dikla was more mellow and before I knew it the 90 minutes had vaporated. I'd slipped into the zone where time flew by and my mind ran free.

The next morning I was eager to start again. I focused my attention on Dikla's instruction and realized that her insistence on form was to prevent injury. She worked with me on a head stand set up and it struck me that I wanted to do one. I would do one. I'd never experienced determination like that. I just knew it would happen.

That afternoon I was curled up to read in one of the open-air bungalows when Dikla walked by with her dog. She spotted me and came over. "How are you?" she asked. "Good! You?" I said. She stopped. "No," she said, "how are you?"

Damn, I thought. *This bitch ain't playin.*

I smiled and said "I'm ok. I'm tired but thankful to be here." We talked a little more. Before I knew it, I had told her about everything that had happened the year before. I explained that I'd planned this trip around the anniversary of Bill's death. She grew serious and said that was amazing for doing what I was doing and that she hoped I would find strength and peace.

Zanzibar was green, lush, tropical. I spent my time exploring the shoreline of the Indian Ocean, losing myself in yoga, and checking out Stone Town, the old section of Zanzibar City. Freddie Mercury was born there and there were several tributes to him around town. I went to the Mercury Museum and noticed that they left out that his death was caused by AIDS. According to the museum, he simply died. Just like that.

The winding streets were crammed with vendors catering to tourists. I loved the brightly colored fabrics and carved jewelry, but the spice endors drew me in the most. I didn't know if it was legal to bring back pices but I loaded up.

Zanzibar had been conquered, in turn, by Omanis and Yemenis and ater by Portuguese and British. Its location made it a key trading port in he Indian Ocean, linking together Arab and African trade routes. It was major site for the East African slave trade, and while I was there I went o the East African Slave Trade Exhibit where the slave market had once tood.

It was difficult to leave history in its own portal and return to a etreat on the other side of the island. The impact of Arab and European nperialism still permeated Zanzibar: Africans were the workers, and white uropeans made up the majority of the tourists. It was uncomfortable to ealize that I was part of that dynamic.

Since yoga was in the mornings and evenings, my afternoons were open to explore the island. I booked a tour of a local forest populated with indigenous red colobus monkeys and a mangrove swamp. I had never seen monkeys free and out in the open before and I loved watching how they interacted with each other and the visitors. It was encouraging to see that Zanzibar took its eco-tourism seriously.

I realized that some of the other visitors had visited before and had come back just for Dikla. She had a little fan club and I was unabashedly a member. Most of the other women were also traveling solo. It was fantastic to congregate together at meal time and swap stories. Dikla would often join us and I loved listening to her talk.

By far the best part of the entire trip was my last evening of yoga. After six days of intense daily classes in the tropical heat and humidity, my body and mind aligned with my goal and, with Dikla's help, I managed to get up into a headstand. Was it perfect? Nope. But I did it. I felt like I had conquered Everest. That evening we all had dinner together, a long table of about 12 of us. A few tight hugs, a few exchanges of phone numbers and social media contacts, and I returned to my room, sad to know that I might never see any of these amazing women again.

My short visit to Stone Town hadn't been enough. I wanted more time here, so I decided to check out of the resort a day early and stay in the city. I found a beautiful boutique hotel and waited with a young couple to check in. They were also American, one from New York and the other from Los Angeles. The boyfriend wore a dashiki, and a few questions revealed that they were both flight attendants. Zanzibar marked his 45th country and her 3rd. I was in awe of them.

The hotel was another highlight of the trip. It was elegantly decked out, with elaborately carved wooden door frames, tiled tubs, and rooms scented with bowls of cloves.

After some exploration and a heavenly dinner, I went up to my room, reveled in a deep bath, and fell asleep reading.

The morning came early with the call to prayer. The building next door was a mosque, so call was loud. Much like in Morocco, I loved how it reverberated throughout my body. I was happy to be up and ready to go, because my next stop was Dar es Salaam.

When I was in my early 20s in New York City, I worked for a fraudulent art dealer named Jacques. Jacques's office was in his apartment and he spent all day stumbling around in his bathrobe yelling "PUTAIN!" at me. My only colleague was a gay man from Brooklyn named Mitch. Mitch had th

thickest skin I'd ever seen and was impervious to Jacques's abuse.

Mitch was super adventurous and loved Zanzibar and Dar es Salaam

traveling to both on a regular basis. After one trip, he'd brought me back

small painting that I still had framed. Dar es Salaam had stuck with me eve

since. The name alone seemed unlike anywhere I'd ever been and I wa

excited to spend a few days there.

Dar was a cooler than Paje had been, which was a relief. I grabbed a tax

to my hotel and the young driver asked me if I was going to be staying for

while. I said just a few days and he gave me his number in case I needed

driver for anything. I immediately took him up on it and we arranged for hir

to spend the next day with me, driving me to some of his recommende

shops, neighborhoods, and the Village Museum.

The highlight of Dar was getting to meet up with a friend from home

Godfrey and I had been in graduate programs at the same time and w

met the day he defended his dissertation. We had become friends an

had dinner together a view times before eventually losing touch. When

remembered that he was from Dar es Salaam and had since moved back,

contacted him and asked if he would be around. He met me at my hotel an

we caught up over beers. It was perfect and I was so thankful to see him.

went back to my room that night thrilled to be exactly where I was.

The next afternoon had me on the move again, this time back to Addis Ababa. I'd booked myself a few days there before going back to California. I arrived at my hotel in the evening, when most of the shops had already closed. As I got out of the taxi, a man smoking out in front commented "I love those shoes!" "Thank you!" I replied. "Is that an American accent I hear?" he asked. "Yes, from California." "I'm from the other side – New Jersey." I mockingly rolled my eyes and said, "It figures." He burst out laughing and said "Well, I was pleased to meet you but I don't know about that now!"

I checked in and dropped off my bags before heading back downstairs in search of dinner. I was ravenous, but it looked like the only thing open nearby was a sports bar. I noticed my New Jersey compatriot was inside and the moment he saw me, he invited me to join him. Ketan was originally from Dar es Salaam but had lived in New Jersey for a decade before recently relocating to Dubai with his wife and son. He had a fantastic sense of humor and we had a great time, cracking each other up over a few drinks. We agreed to grab dinner again if time allowed.

One of my mother's friends was from Addis and had sent me a list of her must-sees. Addis is huge, much bigger than Dar es Salaam, so I booked a tour instead of trying to negotiate it by myself. The driver picked me up at my hotel and an Australian couple joined us. We started with Holy Trinity Church, listening to the otherworldly chants of the priests. From there we went to the National Museum before having lunch at a traditional restaurant, where my tour-mates asked for "just chips, please" instead of the amazing spread in front of us.

Next we went to Mount Entonto, the highest peak in the Entonto mountains at almost 10,500 feet above sea level. Our guide noted that Ethiopian runners train for marathons there because the air is so thin. Addis itself is about 7,700 feet above sea level, making it one of the highest capital cities in the world. This hadn't occurred to me beforehand, but after visiting Entonto I was absolutely exhausted from the altitude. The tour hadn't been particularly stressful or hurried, but I settled back into the van and almost fell asleep. As we crept through the chaos of the Mercato I was thankful to be apart from it all.

After Entonto we made our way to Café Tomoca, which is considered the gold standard of Ethiopian coffee. I'm not a big coffee drinker, but it was the perfect pick-me-up. Despite Tomoca's fame, there were plenty of locals hanging out and chatting over espressos instead of tourist groups clogging up the space.

Our last stop was at the Red Terror Martyrs Memorial Museum, which was a very somber way to end the day. In the late 1970s, an estimated 00,000 to 750,000 men, women, and children were tortured and murdered by Mengistu Haile Miriam's military campaign during one of the darkest times in modern history. I'd never heard of the massacre before and was shaken to my core by it.

Back at the hotel, I was beat. I texted Ketan that I wasn't up to go out or dinner and instead grabbed a nibble at a place around the corner. I passed out early with that familiar feeling of regret settling in. After so much movement and travel over the last year, I wanted more time everywhere. But it was time to return home.

The next day, Ethiopia Airlines sent me an email to bid for an upgrade o first class. Since I'd spent far less on the trip than I'd allocated, I lowballed bid to see what would happen. I was flying home on March 7th, one year o the day since Bill died. Plus, the flight from Addis Ababa to California was 22 hours long. If any time called for an upgrade, it was then. My bid was accepted, which I realized was an indication that COVID-19 cancellations were already starting. I began hoping to make it home without any major interruptions.

On my way to Africa two weeks earlier, the Addis airport had been breeze to get through. Leaving was a different story. The terminals wer mobbed, and airport workers randomly scanned temperatures withou rhyme or reason. Instead of an organized line for my flight there was crowd of people pushing to get through. It was chaos. A couple in front me was scrambling to break down their stroller while wrangling three sm children as the crowd yelled at them to hurry up. I helped them fold th stroller. The mother looked close to tears.

Once on the plane, first class was spread out. Everyone moppe down their trays with tons of sanitizer and I felt foolish that it hadn't eve occurred to me. We weren't up to facemasks just yet, but everyone was edge.

Reality hit at the Washington Dulles airport. Never once ha connecting at Dulles been a pleasant experience, and I braced myself fo hours of waiting at passport control. Instead, we deboarded into a near empty terminal. I was through passport control and customs in 15 minute COVID-19 shutdowns were no joke and they were only beginning.

One week later, California called for shelter-in-place. Peop scrambled to get home before borders closed completely. Several frienc ɔked "Did you bring back the virus?" At that point, Africa had the lowest

COVD-19 numbers in the world.

But that would change too.

21

Eric had moved into the new place while I was away. When I got back, I began to split my time between the new cottage and my old apartment. I still needed to pack up my stuff and clean everything, but it was so good to build a home with him and start our life together. It was also jarring, after a year of constant movement and solitude, to be so totally locked into one place. The shutdowns meant we couldn't go out to eat, we couldn't go to the movies, we couldn't visit friends – none of the usual rituals of a new relationship were possible. Instead, we were thrown together all the time and left to find out if we would sink or swim.

Nothing much changed at work except that the San Francisco office closed and everyone started working remotely. I had been remote since August anyway, so it was all the same to me at first.

But then more and more states shuttered brick and mortar shops, and we absolutely exploded with online orders. Each day was busier than the one before and soon my team was stretched thin. I kept asking to hire more people, but didn't get the greenlight for nearly a month while the company renegotiated some contracts. When they finally DID give me the go-ahead, I was told to double my team and get them trained as quickly as possible. By myself.

My heart sank. The past year had been so fucking stressful and I couldn't even think about adding more to it, but there was nothing I could do. Meanwhile my gym closed, as did my yoga studio, meaning that I lost the activities I'd put in place to create new structure for my life. Once again, things I had so carefully built vanished into thin air.

At least Eric and I were together and had each other for support. Now that we had a stable place to stay, I also started to seriously consider adopting a dog. I wanted a larger dog that would like to hike and would get along with Ichi. But every dog I inquired about turned out to have already been adopted. I was heartbroken each time, but soon had to put my search on hold because I was working so much.

The end of March was a black hole. I was completely absorbed by work and there was no end in sight. My team was exhausted. I was exhausted. We couldn't go anywhere or do anything, and every day we saw higher numbers.

I had just enough in my savings account to sign up for the coaching certification program. I knew it was crazy to add my load, but I needed a bright spot.

By late March it looked like my house was finally going to close. My

eal estate agent called me and explained that the sale was contingent
n three others, before assuring me that once the first closed the others
vould "fall like dominos." I got more nervous with every passing day and
hecked in with her constantly. I knew that with the pandemic raging
here would be very few buyers if we had to put it back on the market.
ventually I got word that the first sale had closed. We were set to finalize
urs within the week. I just needed my sale to go to title.

And then someone fucked up and didn't bring it to title in time. It was
 long weekend, so the office didn't reopen for four days, by which time
he entire sale could fall through. I lost my shit. I knew it wasn't my agent's
ault, or even the title officer's fault, but I didn't care. My mind spun with
verything that was going wrong.

I drove to the ocean and wept in my car for a half hour. I knew I
vas overreacting, but I couldn't handle the pressure anymore. Despite
verything I'd attempted to do, the lack of closure felt like I would never
et out of the place where I'd gotten stuck. What more could I give? I
ad no energy left to think about backup plans. I had no energy left for
 nything at all.

22

On April 5th, I adopted a chihuahua mix named Chica. We drove two and half hours to meet her and found a terrified little being who'd been in foster care for a third of her young life. She was only a year and a half but had already had a litter of puppies. Her foster family didn't know if she was house trained because she slept outside in a kennel. I adopted her on the spot.

It was a long drive back to Cambria. Chica was nestled in next to me and fell asleep. Eric and I tried to come up with a new name for her but none seemed to fit. When we arrived home, I took her for a short walk and it hit me: Fiona. She was Fiona.

Ichi was not particularly enamored with her new little sister, but I was completely in love. She was skittish and we knew we had our work cut out for us. But she slept through the night with no issues and knew to go to the back door when she had to go out. She was a gift to me at a dark time and I adored her.

I soon signed up for another coaching program specific to widows. My vision was becoming clearer: I wanted to help other young widows make it through the awful days after losing their spouse by teaching a focus on physical and emotional health. Whenever I thought back to June and July, I saw that I had been naïve to think that I'd made it through when I had so much more ahead. If I could help even one person in a similar situation, it would all have been worth it.

Was that wrong to say? I didn't care. Bill wasn't coming back; Klaus wasn't coming back. Our life was done. All I could do was help other people feel a little less hopeless too.

By mid-April, work was insane. We had hired over 20 new people and showed no signs of slowing down. I began to throw new hires together with more seasoned workers for training. Some of the newcomers had lost their hospitality jobs to COVID and were overqualified for the position. The one bright spot was that I could hire several acquaintances. They wouldn't be making as much as they had been, but at least we could provide something for the foreseeable future.

Managing 50 people began to take its toll on me. My days were spent scheduling and putting out fires. My job no longer had anything to do with wine. I knew how lucky I was to be employed at all, but every new crisis drained me further. Many of our customers made demands that were impossible at any time, let alone during a pandemic.

My team was tapped out, and I was having an increasingly difficult time cheering them on.

As predicted, our trip to Sicily was cancelled. I knew it was coming, but Claudia was heartbroken. She hadn't travelled much and had been looking forward to meeting up. We had been such supports for each other after Matt and Bill died, and we wanted time to catch up and relax. But it wasn't meant to be.

Eric was still going to work as normal because winemaking was considered an essential job, so Fiona became my constant companion. She gave me an excuse to step away from the computer several times a day. I loved our morning walks and our break at noon. She was growing more confident and comfortable and would snuggle into my lap while I was working. She was the opposite of what I had been looking for, but she was perfect. We needed each other.

April evaporated. The rain stopped but there was nowhere to go. Fear began to reach an all-time high in the country and it was about to burst open.

By the end of April, my house had closed. I breathed a sigh of relief that I would never have to think about it again. With the money I set up accounts for Leah's kids and re-arranged some funds so that I had cash available for a down payment if I was ever fool enough to attempt owning again. I also took a few crash courses in financial literacy.

My coaching program was set to begin around the same time and I couldn't wait to get started. It wasn't the answer to everything, but I hoped it would at least be an interesting experience. A friend from New York also happened to sign up for the same program, so I knew one other person going into it. Finally, my life felt like it had some focus and meaning again.

magic

/'majik/

noun

the power of apparently influencing the course of events by using mysterious or supernatural forces.
"suddenly, as if by magic, the doors start to open"

○ mysterious tricks, such as making things disappear and appear again, performed as entertainment.

"the magic of the theater"
something that has a delightfully unusual quality.

"their seaside town is pure magic"

adjective
used in magic or working by magic; having or apparently having supernatural powers.
"a magic wand"

○ very effective in producing results, especially desired ones.
"confidence is the magic ingredient needed to spark recovery"

phrases
like magic — remarkably effectively or rapidly.
"it repels rain like magic"

23

As Eric and I settled in, we kept ourselves busy with work and with setting up our home.

If we have to be on lockdown, I thought, I'm glad it's here.

When I wasn't working, I threw myself into cooking. One of the many things I missed about Bill was his bread. He was a trained chef, but baking was his first culinary love and he used to bake all of our bread. On our trip to Germany I had discovered that I loved German grain bread, so he figured out a way to make his own. His favorite, though, was sourdough. He could sniff bread at a restaurant and know just how much sourdough was used with what kind of flour. It was quite the party trick.

I had let his sourdough starter die the year before. It never occurred to me to keep it going because I was so overwhelmed. I knew that he'd given some to friends and family over the years, so I sent out a desperate S.O.S. on social media. I couldn't locate any, but a friend in San Francisco overnighted me some of hers and I used it to make my first sourdough loaf. I was nervous as hell and Eric kept teasing me. But to me, it wasn't just bread - it was symbolic of everything I'd lost. I wanted so badly to have a connection to my former life.

By the end of the month, the stress of work got to be too much and Eric and I planned a mental health day. We wanted to take Ichi and Fiona to a nearby creek. We had gone before, but it had been a Saturday and the trails were crowded. Fiona freaked out and barked hysterically at anything and everything, and we left right away.

The next time, we went mid-week and gave Fiona a little CBD to help her relax. No one else was there and Fiona went wild – I let her off the leash and she tore around, leaping and jumping with joy. She was a different dog and my heart leapt along with her. I loved seeing her so happy.

In the year after I lost Bill, I dreaded significant dates and holidays. Thanksgiving had been tough because Bill used to go all out with the cooking. Christmas was also hard, especially so close to our anniversary. The anniversary of his death was brutal, which was why I was mid-air for it. But the one that probably hurt the most was June 5th. Our first date had been on June 5th, even though we didn't know it was a date at the time. We were just two friends going out to dinner. Every year after, though, we celebrated it. When we adopted Klaus we made it his official birthday. Thinking about my first June 5th without them made me nauseous with grief.

But the week leading up to it was amazing. I had been struggling to old things together, and then out of the blue Leah sent me some of Bill's ourdough starter. It arrived a few days before the 5th. I was thrilled to e able to make bread in his honor, with HIS starter. I named the starter andalf, after the lunatic who first taught Bill to make bread so many ecades ago.

Later that week, my brother texted me a picture of an inscription Bill ad made on a book he'd given him. Then one of Bill's high school friends exted me pictures of Bill from back in the day and Bridget told me that e had been on her mind all week. Finally, a former culinary student of ill's messaged me out of nowhere to let me know she was thinking of me. one of them knew the significance of the date. All of them reaching out elt like Bill letting me know that he hadn't forgotten about the importance f the day.

The bread-baking mission sent Eric and me into homesteading verdrive. By the time summer arrived, we hadn't bought bread from the tore in months. Eric learned how to make homemade mustards and jerky or himself and the girls. I made a tofu cheese and looked up recipes from ny travels: feroce d'avocat from Zanzibar, oeufs en meurette from Paris, and fish chowder from Bermuda. We explored flavors from all over the place and made vegetarian versions of old standards. Eric built raised garden beds so we'd have our own produce.

Although I wasn't going to the gym, I didn't gain any weight because was so active around the house. I was also skipping any processed food in favor of what we made ourselves. I began to notice how much better felt physically.

As I progressed in my coaching programs, I felt confident that I' made the right choice by enrolling. It was nerve-wracking at first, bu drawing from my own experience helped me navigate unexpecte situations. I loved working through thought patterns and emotions in m practice sessions.

However, I soon realized I would need to make a decision. Work wa so draining that I couldn't focus on my studies, but whenever I considere leaving my job I panicked at the thought of not having a reliable income. felt caught between the two, trapped into inertia again.

I reached out to a travel website that I had written for the previou fall and asked if they needed contributions. The owner replied right awa that yes, he'd love for me to jump back in. Later the same week, Eric an were in town and saw that one of our favorite shops had a small help wanted sign. I talked to the owner and she was thrilled to have me work one day per week.

And then my financial planner emailed me and wanted to go over my accounts.

Now that the house was settled, I knew I had enough liquid cash to hold me over but I didn't want to blow through it all. I wanted to know if leaving my full-time job would also mean sacrificing my retirement. After a long talk with my planner he assured me that yes, I could take the leap if I really wanted to.

I mulled it over a bit more, and then I got an email from our CEO. He talked about the record numbers we'd been pulling in before saying that "planning for peak starts now." I almost wept. We were all so exhausted from keeping up with demand that I couldn't even begin to think about staffing up for the holidays. It was too much.

Still, I planned to stick it out a bit longer and give notice in August – until my boss, Joe, told me he'd be out for the second part of his paternity leave from mid-July to the end of August. I counted the weeks: if I were to allow him enough time to either hire someone or promote someone before he left, I had to give notice right away.

So I did.

"You're pretty burnt out, aren't you?" he asked.

"Yes. Completely."

"Managing this many people would burn anyone out..."

"Yes."

Joe ran through a few different scenarios to alleviate some pressure and asked if any of them would make me consider staying.

I appreciated it, but I knew that if I stayed on the team would revert back to where it had been.

Then Joe asked "Would you be willing to stay on part time as a coach?"

I was floored. Joe knew I was taking some classes but he didn't know what they were about. I leapt at the opportunity to drop to part-time. felt like a new person.

I started to develop my coaching program in earnest. I had sent out a few feelers and several people replied. Two in particular were eager to start. It was perfect because their personality styles were so different. Both of them challenged me to stretch myself and think through each weekly session in detail beforehand. It's normal for clients to cancel when things get uncomfortable, but both of them continue to show up on time, every time, and tell me how much they looked forward to our sessions. Neither of them was working on grief specifically, but it felt so good to help them let go of habits that were no longer serving them. It felt right.

My home felt right. My life with Eric felt right. My direction felt right. For the first time in a year and a half, I was completely content.

It felt right. It all did.

24

It's been a year since both Bill and Klaus left and it's still so difficult for me to wrap my mind around. It feels like there's a parallel universe somewhere in which we're all still a happy family, living together in the house we loved so much. Bill has retired and I work remotely and life is unfolding just as it should.

But I no longer live in that universe. Their deaths punched me out of it and into this one.

Before Bill died, he was very much a believer in a higher power and I very much was not. While I haven't found God in Bill's absence, I will say now that all I know for sure is that I know nothing.

I don't know what comes next, but I feel so much more at peace with the universe and with my own place within it. I'm part of it and it's a part of me. I never had that understanding before. The cosmic punch that sent me out of our life and into this one knocked that understanding into me.

Bill lived, and he loved his life. I wish we could have stayed together longer, but how can I be sad for him? He lived big, he loved even bigger, and he left when it was time to. He never had to experience complete physical degradation and will forever be his smiling, loving self to me.

I am not at peace with death but I am at peace with myself and that is always the bigger war anyway.

I am free – completely, wildly free. I always was but I never knew it until I lost everything. None of our attachments exist. Even something as fundamental as a marriage is a manufactured state. Our marriage was wonderful, but only because we both recognized it as a gift and treated it as such.

I feel like I've woken up from a lifelong sleep and I see everything so much more clearly. I am comfortable with the unknown and it does not frighten me.

There are moments in which the wave of grief still overwhelms me. I don't see how it could be otherwise. But I don't fight against it. I let myself break down and cry and steep in all of the memories. How could I not? But experiencing that when it needs to happen reminds me of what a goddamn gift our life was. And is.

And who knows? Maybe something will punch me out of this life I'm building with Eric and the girls and back into my previous life. Maybe I'll come home from work one day to find Bill teaching Klaus a new trick. I'll wonder if this has all been a dream.

Either way, it's fucking beautiful.

acknowledgments

We're only as good as the people in our lives and I'm so so so fortunate to have an abundance of amazing people around me.

I first need to thank my mother June Johnson for holding me up and reminding me to bathe during those first few days. I appreciate your list-making abilities now more than ever. I also want to thank my brother Dylan, my sister-in-law Ai, my nephew Nico, my aunt Patty, my cousins Ron and Wendy and the rest of the Johnson clan. You all rock and I'm thankful we're blood.

A huge thank you to Jaci Ianello. You know why.

Thank you to Leah, Casey, Lili, Neva, and little Bill. I know you miss him profoundly. Thank you also to the extended Metzgar, Deiner, and Krepp families. You have no reason to stay in touch with me other than out of your love for Laura and for Bill. Thank you for being so welcoming. And thank you to Beverly for showing such generosity and grace when I hadn't.

Thank you to the Busas for making the side-trip to my place in Oakland and providing that family love that only Italians can.

Thank you to Emanuel Hermellin for answering my calls in the middle of the night and for opening your home to me time and again. You're a gem and should stop scheduling meetings you don't want to attend.

Thank you to Claudia Gallo for your friendship for wayyyy too long and for being my unfortunate sister in grief. You'll always be June's favorite daughter.

Thank you to Rebecca Rodriguez for showing up, ordering food, and eating it all.

Thank you to Claire Stengle for coming all the way to California when your own heart couldn't take any more pain.

Thank you to my little rum ham Bridget O'Malley and to the fooligans Ji & Tim Meunzner, Anne Piorkowski, Tracey Maciejewski, and Kathy & Matt Fenski. I love you all and don't know how I would have made it through last year without you.

Thank you to Dominic Swinn and Nicole Pittman. You two. My god. The best.

Thank you to Tommy Donahoe. Klaus and Dante knew we should be friends. They were right. Here's to Bill, Mickey, and Klaus out there traversing the cosmos.

Thank you to Laora Sullins for being calm and level-headed when I wasn't and for making an absolutely brutal task a little less so.

Thank you to Brother James Doyle for stalking me with love.

Thank you to Brian Minahan for... everything. Always.

Thank you to Jeff Phillips for being a rock on the worst night of my life. The last place anyone wants to be is at work when they get the call, but I'm thankful you were there. Thank you also to Joe Kennedy, Irene Jimu, Katy Simanski, Maisie Lyman, Marcella Newhouse, Andrew Fegelman, and the entire Recs team.

hank you to Charles Springfield for your advice, guidance, and ncouragement. Thank you to Jemma Jorel for planting the seed and to bby Spindleman for the reality check.

hank you to George Rosett for polishing up my coal. I think my favorite omments began with "Fuck!."

hank you to Maria Pabico LaRotonda for making it all legible and look ke something someone might want to read.

hank you to everyone in the coaching programs, but Curtis Eaton in articular. And thank you to my two practice clients who shall remain ameless. You know who you are and how much I appreciate your trust nd honesty.

hank you to Dikla, Jyoti, Lena, and Carsten. You're all gems and our aths crossed for a reason.

oo many other friends to thank so here's a general "I love you all!"

nd thank you to Eric Mohseni for opening first your home and then your eart to me. You're a beautiful soul and I'm so fortunate to have you in my fe. I love you and Ichi and Fiona more than you know.

Made in the USA
Coppell, TX
27 January 2021